Renal Diet Cookbook
2021 Edition

163 Easy, Wholesome, Mouthwatering Recipes that Include Sodium, Potassium and Phosphorous Amounts. With Vegetarian Dishes!

Sabrina Sharp

Contents

INTRODUCTION

It is important to eat a wide variety of foods to stay healthy and strong. If you have kidney issues, then you are also advised to change your diet so as to consume smaller quantities of potassium, sodium, and phosphorous. This diet is referred to as the *renal diet*. Since everyone is different, patients with malfunctioning kidneys will have different dietary requirements to abide by. Speak to a renal dietitian (a diet and nutrition consultant for people with kidney disease) to find a meal plan that works for you. A kidney-friendly diet will also help you protect your kidneys from further damage.

CHAPTER 1. BREAKFAST RECIPES

1.1 Easy Turkey Breakfast Burritos

Preparation time: 30 mins

Servings: 8

Ingredients

- 1 lb. ground turkey meat
- 8 burrito shells
- 2 tbsps. olive oil
- 8 eggs, beaten
- 1/4 cup sliced onions
- 1/4 cup fresh, chopped (green,
- yellow, or red) bell peppers
- 1 tbsp. jalapeño peppers, seeded
- 3 tbsps. fresh scallions, sliced
- 2 tbsps. fresh coriander, chopped
- 1/2 tsp. chili powder
- 1/2 tsp. smoked paprika
- 1 cup cheddar cheese, grated

Nutritional facts per serving

- Calories: 406cal
- Fat: 23g
- Sodium: 514mg
- Protein: 24g
- Potassium: 286mg
- Phosphorus: 360mg
- Carbohydrates: 22g

Steps

- Place the meatloaf, peppers, coriander, onions, and scallions in a pan with 1 tbsp. of olive oil and allow them to cook until the onion becomes transparent. Stir in the spices, and then turn off the flame.
- Set another broad pan over a medium-high flame and add 1 tbsp. olive oil. When heated add the eggs and scramble until set.
- Place the desired quantities of the meatloaf blend, eggs, vegetables, and cheese in the burrito shells. Fold them and serve immediately.

1.2 Instant Omelet

Preparation time: 40 mins

Servings: 1

Ingredients

- 2 eggs
- 2 tbsps. water
- 1 tbsp. unsalted butter
- 1/2 cup seafood, meat, or vegetables

Nutritional facts per serving

- Calories: 256cal
- Fat: 14g
- Sodium: 144mg
- Protein: 12g
- Potassium: 123mg
- Phosphorus: 196mg
- Carbohydrates: 1g

Steps

- Beat the eggs and water together until they are properly blended.
- Heat butter in a 10-inch-long omelet pan or frying pan until it is hot.
- Pour the egg mixture into the pan.

- Check the sides and edges of the egg once it appears to solidify and then use a pancake turner to flip the egg.
- If desired, proceed to add cooked beef, seafood, or a half cup of vegetables to the omelet.
- Fold the omelet in half using the pancake turner. Then, slide the omelet off the pan and onto a plate to serve.

1.3 Blueberry Muffins

Preparation time: 30 mins

Servings: 12

Ingredients

- 1/2 cup unsalted butter
- 1 1/4 cups sugar
- 2 eggs
- 2 cups milk
- 2 cups all-purpose flour
- 2 tsps. baking powder
- 2 1/2 cups fresh blueberries
- 2 tsps. sugar (for the topping)

Nutritional facts per serving

- Calories: 276cal
- Fat: 10g
- Sodium: 210mg
- Protein: 5g
- Potassium: 122mg
- Phosphorus: 101mg
- Carbohydrates: 45g

Steps

- Mix the sugar and butter until they are smoothly blended together, utilizing a low-speed mixer.
- Add the eggs one at a time and keep whisking until they are combined.
- Combine the dry ingredients and mix them in with the other ingredients. Then, stir in some milk.
- Mash and stir in half a cup of blueberries. Then, add the remaining blueberries and mix them by hand.
- Spray the muffin cups with cooking spray and put them in the tin cups.

- Pour the muffin mixture into each muffin cup and sprinkle the muffin tops with honey.
- Bake for 25 to 30 minutes at 375°F. After confirming they are fully cooked, allow them to cool in a pan for at least 30 minutes.

1.4 Stuffed Breakfast Muffins

Preparation time: 25 mins

Servings: 12

Ingredients

- 2 cups flour
- 1 tbsp. sugar or honey
- 1/2 tsps. baking powder
- 1 tbsp. lime juice
- 8 tbsps. soft, unsalted butter
- 3/4 cup milk

Filling

- 4 eggs
- 8 oz. low-sodium bacon (11⁄4 sliced)
- 1 cup cheddar cheese, shredded
- 1/4 cup spring onions, sliced thinly

Nutritional facts per serving

- Calories: 331cal
- Fat: 24g
- Sodium: 329mg
- Protein: 11g
- Potassium: 153mg
- Phosphorus: 171mg
- Carbohydrates: 20g

Steps

- Preheat the oven to 425°F.

Prepare the filling

- Slightly under-cook the scrambled eggs.
- Fry the bacon until crispy.
- Add the remaining ingredients.

Prepare the dough

- Combine all the dry ingredients in a large container.
- Split with a pastry cutter or fork the unsalted butter till pea-size or small.

- In the middle of the blend, make a well, in the milk and lime juice and mix well.
- Start preparing the muffin tins by gently coating them with flour.
- Pour a little of the mix into each tin, then some filling, then again, some mix.
- Bake for 10/12 minutes or until they turn golden brown at 425°F.

1.5 Marshmallow Stuffing Chocolate Pancakes

Preparation time: 30 mins

Servings: 12

Ingredients

Filling

- 1 tbsp. unsweetened ground cocoa
- 1/4 cup heavy cream
- 1/2 cup melted cream cheese
- 1/2 cup marshmallow cream

Pancakes

- 1 cup flour
- 3 tbsps. sugar
- 3 tbsps. cocoa powder unsweetened
- 1/2 tsp. baking powder
- 1 tbsp. lime juice
- 1 egg
- 1 cup milk
- 2 tbsps. olive oil
- 2 tsps. vanilla extract
- 2/3 cup banana protein powder

Nutritional facts per serving

- Calories: 195cal
- Fat: 10g
- Sodium: 121mg
- Protein: 8g
- Potassium: 135mg
- Phosphorus: 135mg
- Carbohydrates: 23g

Steps

Marshmallow filling

- Beat the heavy cream and cocoa together until they form stiff peaks.
- Whisk it for another minute and then add the marshmallow cream, and cream cheese. Cover and put in the refrigerator.

Pancakes

- In a large container, combine all the dry ingredients together and set them aside.
- In a medium-sized bowl, combine all the wet ingredients together.
- Gently fold the dry ingredients into the wet ingredients, refraining from over-mixing.
- Prepare the pancakes at medium-high heat or 375°F on a finely oiled griddle.
- Make sure to flip the pancakes as they begin to bubble.
- Serve with the filling.

1.6 Homemade Buttermilk Pancakes

Preparation time: 10 mins

Servings: 9

Ingredients

- 2 cups all-purpose flour
- 1 tsp. cream of tartar
- 1 1/2 tsps. baking powder
- 2 tbsps. sugar
- 2 cups buttermilk
- 2 large eggs
- 1 tbsp. olive oil and 1/4 cup olive oil (divided)

Nutritional facts per serving

- Calories: 218cal
- Fat: 10g

- Sodium: 330mg
- Protein: 7g
- Potassium: 182mg
- Phosphorus: 100mg
- Carbohydrates: 28g

Steps

- In a wide bowl, mix the dry ingredients together and whisk 1/4 cup olive oil, eggs, and buttermilk.
- Heat a skillet over low heat.
- Add a tbsp. of oil to a pan. Scoop some of the pancake mixture into the skillet using a 1/3 measuring cup. Each pancake should be about 4 inches wide. Use a spatula to flip the pancakes once their edges start to brown and bubbles appear in the middle.
- Set the cooked pancakes aside.
- Serve with fresh berries or scrambled eggs.

1.7 Sirloin Cheddar Quiche

Preparation time: 40 mins

Servings: 6

Ingredients

- 1/2 lb. sirloin steak meat
- 1 cup onions, chopped
- 2 tbsps. canola oil
- 1/2 cup cheddar, shredded
- 5 eggs, beaten
- 1 cup cream
- 1 9" prepared piecrust
- 1/2 tsp. ground black pepper

Nutritional facts per serving

- Calories: 528cal
- Fat: 20g
- Sodium: 393mg
- Protein: 23g
- Potassium: 309mg
- Phosphorus: 282mg
- Carbohydrates: 23g

Steps

- Slice the trimmed sirloin into small pieces.
- Pour some oil in a pan and sauté the sliced steak and onions until the beef is browned.

Put it aside for 10 minutes to allow it to cool slightly. Add the cheese to the pan.
- Beat the eggs and cream in a wide bowl and season with black pepper.
- Spread the steak and cheese mixture onto the piecrust rim. Then, pour over the top of the egg mixture and bake for 30 minutes at 350°F.
- Cover the foil with the cheesesteak quiche and switch the oven off. Enable the quiche to settle for 10 minutes before serving.

1.8 Spicy Tofu Scrambler

Preparation time: 25 mins

Servings: 2

Ingredients

- 1 tsp. olive oil
- 1/4 cup red bell pepper, diced
- 1/4 cup green bell pepper, chopped
- 1 cup solid tofu
- 1 tsp. onion powder
- 1/4 tsp. of garlic powder
- 1 garlic clove, chopped
- 1/8 tsp. turmeric

Nutritional facts per serving

- Calories: 214cal
- Fat: 14g
- Sodium: 25mg
- Protein: 19g
- Potassium: 468mg
- Phosphorus: 243mg
- Carbohydrates: 11g

Steps

- Pour some olive oil into a pan. Then, sauté the garlic and bell peppers in a medium sized, nonstick pan.
- Wash the tofu and place it in the pan while further breaking it with your wooden spoon. Add any remaining ingredients.
- Mix and cook until the tofu becomes a faint golden brown for around 20 minutes on medium heat. Wait until any excess moisture evaporates.
- Serve the tofu scrambler.

1.9 Baked Egg Cups

Preparation time: 25 mins

Servings: 2

Ingredients

- 3 cups cooked rice
- 4 oz. shredded cheddar cheese
- 4 oz. green chilies, diced
- 2 oz. drained and sliced pimentos
- 1/2 cup milk, skimmed
- 2 eggs, beaten
- 1/2 tsp. ground cumin
- 1/2 tsp. black pepper
- Nonstick cooking spray

Nutritional facts per serving

- Calories: 110cal
- Fat: 5g
- Sodium: 80mg
- Protein: 6g
- Potassium: 82mg
- Phosphorus: 92mg
- Carbohydrates: 14g

Steps

- Mix the rice, 2 ounces of cheese, chilies, pimentos, eggs, milk, pepper, and cumin in a wide dish.
- Apply nonstick cooking spray to the muffin cups.
- Split the mixture into the 12 muffin cups. Sprinkle the leftover shredded cheese on top of each cup.

- Bake for 15 minutes at 400°F until the muffins are fully done.

1.10 Baked Eggs with Basil Pesto

Preparation time: 30 mins

Servings: 1

Ingredients

- 2 large eggs
- 1/2 tsp. olive oil
- 1 pack of fresh basil
- 2 tbsps. grated Parmesan cheese
- 1/2 tsp. unsalted sunflower seeds
- 1/2 tsp. lime juice
- 1/2 tsp. lime zest
- 2 tbsps. diced red bell pepper
- 2 tbsps. sliced zucchini
- 2 tbsps. chopped Spanish onions
- 1/4 tsps. cayenne pepper
- 1/2 tsp. fresh chopped garlic

Nutritional facts per serving

- Calories: 309cal
- Fat: 23g
- Sodium: 296mg
- Protein: 21g
- Potassium: 410mg
- Phosphorus: 333mg
- Carbohydrates: 8g

Steps

- Apply cooking spray to the muffin tin.
- Crack an egg into each tin and add a few vegetables on top.
- Season with cayenne pepper.
- Bake for 10/15 minutes at 375°F.
- In the meantime, prepare the pesto in the food processor by pouring in the olive oil, basil, sunflower seeds, parmesan cheese, lemon zest, and lime juice. Pulse until a purée is formed.
- Place a dollop of pesto in the middle when the baked eggs come out of the oven.
- Serve and enjoy.

1.11 Strawberry Applesauce Pancakes

Preparation time: 40 mins

Servings: 4

Ingredients

- 2 cups all-purpose flour
- 1 tsp. cream of tartar
- 1 1/2 tsp. baking powder
- 2 cups rice milk
- 2 large eggs
- 2 tbsps. olive oil
- 2 cups halved strawberries
- 2 cups applesauce, without sugar

Nutritional facts per serving

- Calories: 394cal
- Fat: 6g
- Sodium: 590mg
- Protein: 11g
- Potassium: 451mg
- Phosphorus: 136mg
- Carbohydrates: 70g

Steps

- In a bowl, mix the dry ingredients together.
- In a separate bowl, combine the wet ingredients. Then, slowly combine and whisk together the contents of each bowl.
- Place the frying pan over medium-high heat and add some oil to it. Use a 1/3 measuring cup to scoop out pancake batter into the skillet. When bubbles emerge, flip the pancakes using a spatula. Allow them to brown on the other side.
- Serve with strawberries and applesauce.

1.12 Fruit & Cheese Omelet

Preparation time: 15 mins

Servings: 1

Ingredients

- 2 eggs
- 1 tsp. of water
- 1/4 cup of cottage cheese (low sodium)

- 1/2 canned, drained fruit salad
- Icing sugar (optional)

Nutritional facts per serving

- Calories: 217cal
- Fat: 11g
- Sodium: 129mg
- Protein: 20g
- Potassium: 259mg
- Phosphorus: 209mg
- Carbohydrates: 14g

Steps

- In a shallow cup, mix the eggs and water together.
- Spray a 8-inch nonstick skillet with cooking spray and allow it to heat up. Pour the egg mixture into it and allow the eggs to cook gently.
- Cook the omelet until the eggs are almost settled on the top but still look wet. Spoon the cottage cheese over them with 1/4 cup of fruit salad. Fold the omelet and place it on a tray.
- Place the omelet on a tray and serve with icing sugar (optional).

1.13 Breakfast Burrito

Preparation time: 15 mins

Servings: 2

Ingredients

- Nonstick cooking spray
- 4 eggs
- 3 tbsps. green, diced chilies
- 1/4 tsp. ground cumin
- 1/2 tsp. sweet pepper sauce
- 2 tortillas
- 2 tbsps. Salsa

Nutritional facts per serving

- Calories: 257cal
- Fat: 13g
- Sodium: 385mg
- Protein: 16g
- Potassium: 247mg

- Phosphorus: 185mg
- Carbohydrates: 21g

Steps

- Spray a medium-sized skillet with nonstick cooking oil and heat over a medium/high flame.
- Whisk the eggs in a bowl and mix with the green chili, cumin, and pepper sauce.
- Pour the eggs into the skillet and cook until the eggs become firm, stirring for one to two minutes.
- Heat the tortillas in an oven or a separate pan for 20 seconds.
- Divide the egg mixture between each tortilla and fold it like a burrito.
- Serve each with one tablespoon of salsa.

1.14 Applesauce Mint French Toast

Preparation time: 15 mins

Servings: 2

Ingredients

- 2 eggs, lightly beaten
- 1/8 tsp. mint
- 1/2 cup milk
- 3/4 cup apple sauce
- 1 tsp margarine
- 4 bread slices

Nutritional facts per serving

- Calories: 353cal

- Fat: 9g
- Sodium: 463mg
- Protein: 13g
- Potassium: 255mg
- Phosphorus: 185mg
- Carbohydrates: 61g

Steps

- Mix the eggs, milk, and mint in a cup.
- Add applesauce to the mix.
- Over a medium-high flame, spread a dollop of margarine on a nonstick plate.
- Soak the slices of bread in the egg mixture and cook them over the skillet.
- Flip the bread and sear the other side until the bottom has browned.

1.15 Spinach & Cheese Omelet

Preparation time: 15 mins

Servings: 2

Ingredients

- 10 eggs
- 1 cup ricotta cheese
- 1 tbsp. freshly chopped herbs
- 1 tbsp. olive oil
- 1 medium-sized onion, chopped
- 2 cups of raw spinach

Nutritional facts per serving

- Calories: 221cal
- Fat: 16g
- Sodium: 175mg
- Protein: 17g
- Potassium: 256mg
- Phosphorus: 204mg
- Carbohydrates: 7g

Steps

- Preheat the oven to 350°F.
- In a nonstick, oven-proof plate, sauté the onion in olive oil.
- Add the spinach and sauté.
- Mix together the eggs, ricotta cheese, and fresh herbs in a separate bowl.
- Add the egg mixture to the dish.

- Finish cooking the omelet in the oven (around 10 minutes or until the top sets properly).
- Serve and enjoy.

1.16 Mushroom & Leek Pie

Preparation time: 30 mins

Servings: 8

Ingredients

- 9"-long pre-made pastry shell
- 8 to 10 eggs
- 1/2 cup mushrooms, sliced
- 1/2 cup leeks, sliced
- 1 tbsp. olive oil
- 2 tbsp. grated parmesan cheese
- Black pepper
- Fresh thyme

Nutritional facts per serving

- Calories: 185cal
- Fat: 13g
- Sodium: 167mg
- Protein: 9g
- Potassium: 123mg
- Phosphorus: 102mg
- Carbohydrates: 12g

Steps

- Heat up the oven to 350°F.
- Sauté the cut leeks and mushrooms in one tablespoon of olive oil.
- Season with black pepper and thyme.
- Pour the sautéed leeks and mushrooms on the base of the pastry shell
- Then, whisk together the eggs and cheese and pour in the pastry shell over the leeks and mushrooms
- Bake until it sets, for approximately 30 minutes.

1.17 Lemon Apple Smoothie

Preparation time: 5 mins

Servings: 4

Ingredients

- 1/4 cup lime juice
- 1/2 cup apple juice
- 1 peeled and cored apple
- 1 banana
- 3 tsps. honey
- 1 cup frozen strawberry yogurt

Nutritional facts per serving

- Calories: 171cal
- Fat: 3g
- Sodium: 38mg
- Protein: 3g
- Potassium: 328mg
- Phosphorus: 60mg
- Carbohydrates: 39g

Steps

- Combine all the ingredients in a blender and pulse until they are creamy.
- Pour the smoothie mixture into the glasses.

1.18 Pumpkin Applesauce Bread or Muffins

Preparation time: 30 mins

Servings: 8

Ingredients

- 1/2 cup unsweetened applesauce
- 1 cup brown sugar
- 1/2 cup palm oil
- 2 eggs
- 2 cups all-purpose flour
- 1 tsp. baking soda
- 1/2 tsp. baking powder
- 2 tbsps. pumpkin pie seasoning

Nutritional facts per serving

- Calories: 253cal
- Fat: 1g
- Sodium: 142mg
- Protein: 4g
- Potassium: 83mg
- Phosphorus: 42mg
- Carbohydrates: 39g

Steps

- Preheat the oven to 425°F
- Spray oil across the muffin tins.
- Whisk the brown sugar, applesauce, eggs, and oil together in a medium-sized bowl.
- Mix the remaining items in a single medium-sized container.
- Add the applesauce mixture to the flour and whisk gently until just barely mixed.
- Pour the batter in a muffin pan or loaf.
- Bake for around 50 to 60 minutes if you are making a loaf or for around 20 minutes if you are making muffins.
- Poke a toothpick into a muffin and see if it comes out clean. If it does, proceed to take the muffins out of the oven and allow them to cool.

1.19 Quick Burritos

Preparation time: 10 mins

Servings: 2

Ingredients

- 1/2 tsp olive or canola oil
- 1/2 red bell pepper, thinly sliced
- 4 scallions, thinly sliced
- 8 eggs, beaten
- 4 (6"-long) maize tortillas

Nutritional facts per serving

- Calories: 230cal
- Fat: 14g
- Sodium: 138mg
- Protein: 15g
- Potassium: 212mg
- Phosphorus: 255mg
- Carbohydrates: 14g

Steps

- Heat the oil over low heat in a medium-sized frying pan.
- Add the scallions and bell pepper, sautéing them for around three minutes until tender.
- Add the eggs and mix them until the eggs are thoroughly cooked.
- Place the tortillas between two wet paper towels and put them on a dish.
- Heat the tortillas for two minutes in the oven.
- Spoon the mixture of eggs into the soft tortillas.
- Roll them up to eat.
- Try adding a drop of hot sauce or some chili powder to give it a slight kick.

1.20 Biscuits with Master Mix

Preparation time: 30 mins

Servings: 12

Ingredients

- 3 cups of master mix (check next recipe)
- 2/3 cup of water

Nutritional facts per serving

- Calories: 175cal
- Fat: 2g
- Sodium: 172mg
- Protein: 4g

- Potassium: 82mg
- Phosphorus: 52mg
- Carbohydrates: 19g

Steps

- Preheat the oven to 450°F
- Mix the ingredients together and allow the mixture to stand for five minutes
- Knead the dough about 15 times on a well-floured counter.
- Divide the dough into 12 pieces and shape into biscuits.
- Put the biscuits on a non-oil baking sheet.
- Bake until golden brown for 10 to 12 minutes.

1.21 Master Mix

Preparation time: 10 mins

Servings: 12

Ingredients

- 9 cups all-purpose flour
- 1tbsp. baking powder
- 2 tsps. cream of tartar
- 1 tsp. baking soda
- 1 1/2 cups powdered milk
- 2 1/4 cups vegetable shortening

Nutritional facts per serving

- Calories: 640cal
- Fat: 2g
- Sodium: 271mg
- Protein: 12g
- Potassium: 299mg
- Phosphorus: 190mg
- Carbohydrates: 68g

Steps

- Mix the flour, baking powder, cream of tartar, baking soda, powdered milk and shortening together.
- Store the contents in a cold, dry position in a big, airtight jar.
- Be sure to use it within 10 to 12 weeks.

1.22 Blueberry Pancakes

Preparation time: 20 mins

Servings: 3

Ingredients

- 1 1/2 cups sifted, all-purpose simple flour
- 2 tbsps. baking powder
- 3 tbsps. sugar
- 1 cup buttermilk
- 2 tsps. unsalted margarine
- 2 eggs, lightly beaten
- 1 cup blueberries

Nutritional facts per serving

- Calories: 224cal
- Fat: 7g
- Sodium: 197mg
- Protein: 8g
- Potassium: 129mg
- Phosphorus: 100mg
- Carbohydrates: 36g

Steps

- In a mixing bowl, combine the baking powder, sugar, and flour.
- In the middle, create a well and add the remaining items gradually, steadily mixing throughout to create a thick batter.
- Heat a large 12-inch skillet or griddle and gently oil it.
- Proceed to cook the pancakes, tossing each once bubbles form around the edges.
- Serve immediately.

CHAPTER 2. MAIN COURSES

2.1 Thai Pineapple Prawns & Jasmine Rice

Preparation time: 25 mins

Servings: 8

Ingredients

- 2 3/4 cups uncooked jasmine rice
- 1 1/2 lbs. medium-sized prawns, uncooked
- 1 lime cut in 4 pieces
- 1 can of pineapples
- 2 tbsps. olive oil
- 3/4 cup red onion
- 1 cup cut mushrooms
- 4 cloves garlic
- 1 tsp. hot Sriracha chili sauce
- 3/4 cup fresh mint
- 1/2 cup fresh Thai basil
- 1 tbsp. fresh ginger
- 1/2 cup coconut milk, lite
- 1/2 cup chicken stock, low-sodium
- 1 tbsp. cornstarch
- 1 cup green peas, frozen
- 1/4 tsp. paprika

Nutritional facts per serving

- Calories: 371cal
- Fat: 10g
- Sodium: 226mg
- Protein: 24g
- Potassium: 459mg
- Phosphorus: 283mg
- Carbohydrates: 50g

Steps

- Cook the rice basing on the product's instructions.
- Place the prawns in a bowl and squeeze 2 lime pieces over them before setting them aside for up to 10 minutes.
- Drain the pineapple from its can and put it in a wide bowl. Set it aside.
- Dice the onion, crush the garlic, cut the basil and mint, and grind the ginger.
- Heat one tablespoon of olive oil over a medium-high flame in a frying pan. Add the onion, mushrooms, and three-quarters of the garlic. Fry everything for at least three minutes.
- Proceed to add the prawns and chili sauce, cooking and stirring until the shrimp turns pink. Remove from heat and stir in half a cup of mint as well as the basil and ginger.
- Add the shrimp mixture to the pineapple. Then, squeeze the two remaining limes over the mixture, toss, and set it aside.
- Sauté the remaining quarter-cup of mint and garlic in one tablespoon of olive oil to make the sauce. Add the coconut milk, chicken stock, and cayenne pepper.
- Mix the cornstarch in half a cup of reserved pineapple juice and add it to the sauce, stirring steadily until it thickens over medium-high heat.

- Heat the peas in the microwave for three minutes as the sauce thickens.
- Proceed to mix the sauce and peas with the shrimp and pineapple.
- Serve the jasmine rice with the prawn pineapple sauce. Season with paprika.

2.2 Paprika Chicken with Rice

Preparation time: 30 mins

Servings: 4

Ingredients

- 6 chicken thighs (boneless and skinless)
- 1 1/2 cups frozen peas
- 1 1/2 cups long-grain rice
- 1 large tomato tin, washed and
- chopped
- 1 large-sized onion, thinly sliced
- 1 3/4 cups chicken stock
- 2 tsps. olive oil
- 2 tsps. paprika
- 2 garlic cloves, thinly chopped
- Pepper

Nutritional facts per serving

- Calories: 456cal
- Fat: 12.7g
- Sodium: 820mg
- Protein: 28.7g
- Potassium: 350mg
- Phosphorus: 230mg
- Carbohydrates: 51.7g

Steps

- In a wide pan, heat one tablespoon of olive oil.
- Cook the chicken until it is slightly browned, flipping the pieces every few minutes.
- Add the remaining oil, remove the chicken, and fry the onion and garlic until they soften.

- Mix in the rice and allow the food to simmer for five minutes, stirring continuously.
- Add the peas, paprika, tomatoes, chicken stock, and pepper. Boil it over low heat.
- Place the chicken pieces over the surface of the rice, cover it with foil, and simmer over low heat for at least 25 minutes. The chicken will be properly cooked when the liquid has been completely absorbed and the chicken is no longer pink.

2.3 Roast Lamb

Preparation time: 2 hours

Servings: 4

Ingredients

- 4 lbs. boneless lamb leg, rolled and joined
- 2 tsps. dried and crushed oregano leaves
- 4 tsps. fresh rosemary leaves
- 2 garlic cloves
- 1 tsp. black pepper
- 2 oz. butter
- 2 oz. fresh lemon juice
- 1 cup water

Nutritional facts per serving

- Calories: 318cal
- Fat: 22g
- Sodium: 326mg
- Protein: 30g
- Potassium: 394mg
- Phosphorus: 228mg
- Carbohydrates: 2g

Steps

- Preheat the oven to 320°F. Take out the butter and allow it to reach room temperature.
- Remove the fat from the lamb, cut it, and put it aside in a roasting tray.
- Mince the garlic and dice the rosemary.

- In a shallow cup, mix the rosemary, garlic, oregano, pepper, and half the soft butter.
- Use a sharp knife to cut slits into the leg of the lamb and cram the herb and butter mixture into the slits.
- Slather the remaining herb and butter combination over the lamb.
- Mix the remaining butter with the lemon juice and pour it over the lamb.
- Cover and bake for 2 hours.

2.4 Cauliflower & Chickpea Curry

Preparation time: 30 mins

Servings: 4

Ingredients

- 1/2 lbs. cauliflower, cut into tiny florets
- 1 tbsp. vegetable oil
- 1 small, finely chopped onion
- 1 garlic clove
- 1/2 oz. red lentils
- 2 tsp. garam masala
- 1 cup of chickpeas, drained
- 2 tsps. mango chutney
- 1 tbsp. lime juice
- 1 tbsp. fresh, chopped coriander leaves
- 1 1/2 cups white rice

Nutritional facts per serving

- Calories: 203cal
- Fat: 34g
- Sodium: 406mg
- Protein: 9g
- Potassium: 901mg
- Phosphorus: 190mg
- Carbohydrates: 38g

Steps

- In a pot with boiling water, add the cauliflower florets and allow them to boil for five minutes or until they soften.
- Meanwhile, heat the oil in a wide pan and fry the onion until it softens over medium-high heat. Add 2 cups of water and stir in the garlic, lentils, and garam masala. Let the mixture boil and cook for 20 minutes or until the vegetables and grains soften. Meanwhile, cook the rice.
- Add the chickpeas, boiled cauliflower, lemon juice, mango chutney, and allow the mixture to simmer for five minutes or until fully cooked. Add the fresh coriander leaves for garnishing. Serve with the rice.

2.5 Tandoori-Style Kebabs

Preparation time: 20 mins

Servings: 2

Ingredients

- 2 medium-sized chicken breasts
- Half tin of pure yogurt
- Half a large green pepper
- 1 garlic clove, chopped
- 1/2 medium-sized onion
- 2 tsps. mango chutney
- 2 tsps. curry powder
- 2 pita breads

Nutritional facts per serving

- Calories: 263cal

- Fat: 5g
- Sodium: 163mg
- Protein: 34g
- Potassium: 764mg
- Phosphorus: 328mg
- Carbohydrates: 24g

Steps

- Prepare four metal skewers for the kebab.
- Combine the mango chutney, yogurt, and curry powder together. Proceed to grate the garlic and add it to yogurt mix.
- Cut the chicken into large chunks and add it to the marinade. Leave the chicken to marinate for at least one hour in the fridge. Meanwhile, slice the green pepper and onion into large pieces.
- Place alternating pieces of marinated chicken, onion, and pepper on the four skewers.
- Preheat the grill to medium-high heat and flip the kebabs periodically for five minutes. Serve with pita bread.

2.6 Baked Lamb with Potatoes

Preparation time: 1 hour

Servings: 6

Ingredients

- 2 lbs. lamb leg or shoulder (with
- bone)
- 2 garlic cloves, finely minced
- 1 medium-sized onion, peeled and quartered
- 1 lb. potatoes, peeled and chopped into small pieces
- 1 tbsp. thyme
- 2 bay leaves
- 2 tbsps. olive oil
- 1 pinch ground black pepper
- 1/2 cup water

- 1 cup carrots, peeled and sliced thinly
- 1 cup green peas, frozen

Nutritional facts per serving

- Calories: 379cal
- Fat: 17g
- Sodium: 156mg
- Protein: 20g
- Potassium: 421mg
- Phosphorus: 189m
- Carbohydrates: 35g

Steps

- Preheat the oven to 350°F. Rub the garlic over the lamb.
- Place the sliced onion, carrots, green peas, and potatoes in a baking tray. Add the water and season with the oil, pepper, thyme, and bay leaves. Place the meat over the vegetables and cover.
- Cook for about 2 hours. Before slicing, allow the meat to rest for 15 minutes.

2.7 Homemade Beef Stew

Preparation time: 1 hour

Servings: 4

Ingredients

- 3/4 lb. beef
- 4 cups of potatoes
- 4 cups of carrots
- Half a medium-sized onion
- 1/4 tsp. black pepper
- 1/4 cup flour
- 1/4 cup olive oil

Nutritional facts per serving

- Calories: 360cal
- Fat: 7.5g
- Sodium: 108mg
- Protein: 30g

- Potassium: 421mg
- Phosphorus: 189mg
- Carbohydrates: 19g

Steps

- Coat the meat in flour and pepper.
- In a pot, sauté the coated beef in olive oil. Cover with water and bring to a boil, then add the potatoes, carrots, and onion. Cook until the food becomes tender. Serve immediately.

2.8 Ginger & Soy Short Ribs with Brown Rice

Preparation time: 4 hours

Servings: 4

Ingredients

- 4 chopped carrots
- 2 leeks, well rinsed and chopped
- 6 lbs. beef short ribs
- 1 pinch black pepper
- 1/2 cup beef stock
- 3 oz. sherry
- 2 oz. reduced-sodium soy sauce
- 3 tbsps. honey
- 1 tbsp. vinegar rice
- 1 tbsp. fresh ginger, minced
- 3 garlic cloves, minced
- 4 cups cooked brown rice
- 2 tbsps. fresh coriander leaves, chopped
- 2 spring onions, chopped
- 2 tbsps. pickled jalapeno peppers, minced
- 1 tsp. lime zest

Nutritional facts per serving

- Calories: 290cal
- Fat: 10g
- Sodium: 116mg
- Protein: 20g
- Potassium: 450mg

- Phosphorus: 180mg
- Carbohydrates: 13g

Steps

- Place a large dutch oven, saucepan, or electric slow cooker on the heat and prepare the carrots and leeks.
- Place the ribs, carrots and leeks in the cooker, season with pepper. Mix the soy sauce, stock, honey, sherry, vinegar, garlic, and ginger together in a medium-sized bowl. Pour the mixture over the ribs.
- Cover for three to four hours and braise. Stir in the spring onions, jalapeno peppers, coriander, and lime zest. In the meanwhile, warm the rice.
- Serve the slow-cooked ribs and vegetables with the rice.

2.9 Sweet & Sour Pork

Preparation time: 30 mins

Servings: 2

Ingredients

- 8oz. lean pork, sliced into 1"-long cubes
- 1 tsp. olive oil
- Black pepper
- 1 tsp. ground ginger
- Deep frying oil

Batter

- 6 oz. flour
- 1 small egg
- 1/2 pint water
- 1/2 tsp. oil

Sweet & Sour Sauce

- 2 tbsps. white sugar
- Black pepper
- 6 tbsps. vinegar
- Few drops of red food coloring
- 1/3 pint of water
- 2 tsps. Cornflower
- 2 tbsps. pineapple juice (from canned pineapple tin)

Nutritional facts per serving

- Calories: 250cal
- Fat: 17g
- Sodium: 170mg
- Protein: 32g
- Potassium: 486mg
- Phosphorus: 256mg
- Carbohydrates: 8g

Steps

- Pour some flour into the center of a bowl. Add an egg, water, oil, and stir everything. Allow the mixture to rest for 20 minutes.
- To make sweet and sour sauce, pour the vinegar, spices, pineapple juice, sugar, and water into a saucepan. Bring it to a boil.
- Blend two spoons of cold water with the cornflower, stir it into the sauce, and leave it to simmer for two minutes.
- In a separate bowl, mix the pork cubes, ground ginger, olive oil, and pepper together. Coat the cubes with two teaspoons of flour, removing any excessive flour. Add the batter to the meat. Heat the cooking oil

until it is hot and then add the pork, leaving it to cook until it turns golden brown.
- You may serve the meat with rice.

2.10 Beef Cannelloni

Preparation time: 40 mins

Servings: 4

Ingredients

- Cannelloni, 8 pieces
- 10 oz. of minced beef
- 1 1/2 oz. white breadcrumbs
- 2 oz. grated cheese
- 1 egg, beaten
- 1 pinch of ground nutmeg
- 1 tbsp. beef gravy
- 1 pinch ground black pepper
- 1 oz. butter
- 1/4 pint of water

Nutritional facts per serving

- Calories: 258cal
- Fat: 10g
- Sodium: 279mg
- Protein: 24g
- Potassium: 448mg
- Phosphorus: 253mg
- Carbohydrates: 18g

Steps

- Boil the cannelloni for 8 to 10 minutes, then drain. Break each piece lengthwise and then open it.
- Mix the breadcrumbs, ground beef, egg, nutmeg, and half the cheese together to create the filling. Add a little gravy and then season to taste. Divide the mixture into 8 parts and put into the shells of the cannelloni. Proceed to roll them up like sausages.

- In a shallow, buttered ovenproof bowl, add the cannelloni. Sprinkle with the remaining cheese. Pour 1/2 glass of water into the dish and cook for 25 to 30 minutes in a mild oven at 350°F.

2.11 Sweet & Sour Chicken Stir Fry

Preparation time: 20 mins

Servings: 2

Ingredients

- 1 lb. chicken, sliced into small
- chunks
- 1 tbsp. vegetable oil
- 1 pinch ground black pepper
- 8 oz. mashed canned pineapple
- 2 tsps. lime juice
- 2 tsps. honey
- 1 pinch paprika

Nutritional facts per serving

- Calories: 312cal
- Fat: 3g
- Sodium: 122mg
- Protein: 25g
- Potassium: 237mg
- Phosphorus: 113mg
- Carbohydrates: 11g

Steps

- In a nonstick fry pan, heat some oil and add the chicken with some black pepper. Wait until the chicken turn golden, constantly stirring over a high flame.
- Mix the honey and pineapple together and add them to the pan. Cook them for a further three minutes before stirring in the lemon juice and removing the pan from the heat.

- Serve instantly with paprika as a garnish and boiled rice or pasta.

2.12 Beef Bolognese Sauce

Preparation time: 40 mins

Servings: 4

Ingredients

- 1 lb. minced beef
- 1 tbsp. vegetable oil
- 1 small onion, finely chopped
- 1 garlic clove
- 1/2 oz. corn flour
- 1 cup unsalted beef stock
- 1 pinch black pepper
- 2 tsps. dried oregano
- 7oz. canned tomatoes, chopped and drained

Nutritional facts per serving

- Calories: 242cal
- Fat: 14g
- Sodium: 92mg
- Protein: 22g
- Potassium: 328mg
- Phosphorus: 188mg
- Carbohydrates: 7g

Steps

- Add oil to a frying pan and sauté the onions and the diced garlic briefly.
- Add the beef and stir constantly for 5 minutes before adding the stock. Leave the stock to boil for 20 minutes.
- Season with pepper, and oregano. Then, add some canned (and drained) tomatoes, which you should add and further leave for two minutes to cook.
- Mix a little cool water with the cornflower and add it to the plate, stirring constantly. Simmer for 10 minutes.

2.13 Tuna & Potato Bake

Preparation time: 40 mins

Servings: 4

Ingredients

- 1 lb. potatoes
- 1 medium-sized onion, diced
- 1/2 tbsps. lime juice
- 1 lb. canned tuna fish, drained
- 4 eggs, beaten
- 1 pinch black pepper
- 1 pinch nutmeg
- 1 tsp. butter

Nutritional facts per serving

- Calories: 323cal
- Fat: 18g
- Sodium: 66mg
- Protein: 23g
- Potassium: 454mg
- Phosphorus: 261mg
- Carbohydrates: 15g

Steps

- Sauté the onion and add the diced potatoes, cooking both for 10 minutes.
- Add the beaten eggs, nutmeg, and lime juice.
- Slice the tuna and add to it the potato mixture, which should then be poured into a buttered, ovenproof dish.
- Bake the dish for around 30 minutes in a hot oven at 450°F until the top turns golden.

2.14 Savory Minced Beef

Preparation time: 20 mins

Servings: 4

Ingredients

- 1 lb. minced beef
- 1 tbsp. vegetable oil
- 1 small-sized onion, chopped finely
- 1 cup canned tomatoes, drained
- 1 cup chopped carrots
- 1/2 corn flour
- 3/4 pint unsalted stock
- Pepper
- Parsley for garnish

Nutritional facts per serving

- Calories: 268cal
- Fat: 8g
- Sodium: 154mg
- Protein: 21g
- Potassium: 632mg
- Phosphorus: 270mg
- Carbohydrates: 18g

Steps

- Boil the carrots and put them to the side.
- Sauté the onion in a frying pan until it becomes soft and golden brown.

- Stir in the minced beef and fry until browned.
- Mix in the stock and allow it to boil for two minutes. Add the tomatoes.
- Mix the corn flour with a little cold water and keep stirring it in the pan.
- Add the boiled carrots and simmer for an extra 10 minutes. Add a little extra water if required.
- Season with pepper, garnish with parsley and serve.

2.15 Corned Beef Hash

Preparation time: 40 mins

Servings: 4

Ingredients

- 12 oz. of corned beef
- 1 tsp. of olive oil
- 1 medium onion, peeled and
- chopped
- 1 lb. of boiled potatoes, smashed and seasoned with pepper, milk, and butter.
- 1 tsp. butter

Nutritional facts per serving

- Calories: 368cal
- Fat: 11g
- Sodium: 207mg
- Protein: 29g
- Potassium: 632mg
- Phosphorus: 270mg
- Carbohydrates: 28g

Steps

- Sauté the onion in the oil for around 10 minutes.
- Mix the onion, potatoes, and corned beef together before adding them to a well-buttered, ovenproof bowl. Bake the dish for

approximately 30 minutes in a hot oven at 450°F until the surface browns.

2.16 Lamb Casserole

Preparation time: 30 mins

Servings: 4

Ingredients

- 1 lb. lamb, sliced into 1" cubes
- 6 oz. carrots, sliced
- 5 oz. swede, chopped
- 7 oz. onion, chopped
- 2 oz. canned tomatoes, drained and sliced
- 1 oz. all-purpose flour
- 1 pint unsalted beef stock
- 1 1/2 tbsp. olive oil
- 1 garni bouquet
- 1/2 tsps. dried rosemary
- 1 pinch pepper
- 1 tsp. dried parsley

Nutritional facts per serving

- Calories: 368cal
- Fat: 8g
- Sodium: 154mg
- Protein: 21g
- Potassium: 462mg
- Phosphorus: 270mg
- Carbohydrates: 32.8g

Steps

- Boil the swede for five minutes. Add the onion and carrots and allow the mixture to simmer for a further five minutes.
- Set the veggies to one side. Fry the lamb until it is browned in the vegetable oil. Remove the lamb with a slotted spoon and set it aside. Add the flour and cook to make a roux for two to three minutes.
- Add the stock, constantly stirring, and allow it to simmer for two to three minutes.

Combine the drained, chopped tomatoes, garni bouquet, and rosemary and add to the pan with the lamb. Allow the food to cook over low heat until the lamb becomes tender. adding additional stock or water if required.

- Season with pepper, garnish with parsley and serve.

2.17 Turkey Burgers

Preparation time: 20 mins

Servings: 4

Ingredients

- 1 lb. lean, ground turkey
- 1 cup zucchini, grated
- 1 large egg
- 1/4 cup panko breadcrumbs
- 1/4 cup chopped red onions
- 1 garlic clove
- 1/2 tsp. black pepper
- 1 tbsp. vegetable oil

Nutritional facts per serving

- Calories: 177cal
- Fat: 4g
- Sodium: 99mg
- Protein: 32g
- Potassium: 266mg
- Phosphorus: 63mg
- Carbohydrates: 9g

Steps

- Mix all the ingredients in a large container.
- Shape the patties so that they are of an equal size, around half-an-inch thick.
- Heat one teaspoon of vegetable oil over medium heat in a broad non-stick skillet.
- Fry the patties and lower the heat to a medium, cooking around five minutes per side, until browned.

- Make sure that the patties are fried in the center. Remember to freeze any extras for later use.

2.18 Taco Pockets

Preparation time: 30 mins

Servings: 4

Ingredients

- 8 oz. cooked and shredded chicken
- 1/4 cup sliced red onion
- 2 oz. cheddar cheese, shredded
- 2 pita pockets, 6" in diameter
- 1 tbsp. lime juice
- 1 medium-sized tomato, diced
- 2 tbsps. French dressing for salads
- 1 tbsp. taco sauce
- 1 cup sliced lettuce

Steps

- Mix the cheese, chicken, tomato and onion in a dish.
- Slice the pita in two pieces and spoon one fourth of the mixture into each half of the pita.
- Cover the pieces so that they stay together in foil or parchment paper. Refrigerate before serving.
- In a shallow bowl, mix the dressing with the taco sauce.
- Sprinkle two teaspoons of sauce over the chicken filling in the sandwich and line with lettuce to eat. Keep it in the fridge for three days at a maximum before consuming.

2.19 Cider Cream Chicken

Preparation time: 30 mins

Servings: 8

Ingredients

- 4 chicken breasts
- 2 tbsps. melted butter
- 2 cups half and half
- 3/4 cup apple cider vinegar

Nutritional facts per serving

- Calories: 312cal
- Fat: 15g
- Sodium: 109mg
- Protein: 37g
- Potassium: 370mg
- Phosphorus: 280mg
- Carbohydrates: 8g

Steps

- Place the melted butter in a pan. Add the chicken to the pan and sauté it over a medium-high flame, frying the meat across both sides until it browns.
- Add the vinegar and lower the flame, cooking it for 20 minutes over the stove.
- Remove the chicken from the skillet and keep it warm.
- Add the vinegar and let it boil until it reduces.

- Over the heat, incorporate the half and half and whisk it until it thickens slightly.
- Pour some cream sauce over the chicken.
- Serve and enjoy.

2.20 Pesto Crusted Catfish

Preparation time: 30 mins

Servings: 8

Ingredients

- 2 pounds catfish (filleted and boned)
- 4 tsps. pesto
- 3/4 cup breadcrumbs
- 1/2 cup mozzarella cheese
- 2 tbsps. olive oil

Seasoning

- 1 tsp. garlic powder
- 1 tsp. onion powder
- 1/2 tsp. dried oregano
- 1/2 tsp. red pepper flakes
- 1/2 tsp. black pepper

Nutritional facts per serving

- Calories: 313cal
- Fat: 16g
- Sodium: 273mg
- Protein: 27g
- Potassium: 577mg
- Phosphorus: 418mg
- Carbohydrates: 16g

Steps

- Preheat the oven to 400°F.
- In a small cup, combine the garlic powder, onion powder, oregano, red pepper flakes and black pepper, sprinkle even quantities on both sides of the fish.
- Spread equal quantities of pesto on the top of the fillets (one teaspoon each) and set them aside.

- Mix the breadcrumbs, oil, and cheese in a medium-sized bowl. Apply it to each of the two sides of the fish.
- Add some non-stick cooking spray to the baking sheet on the tray and place the fish on the sheet, leaving room between the fillets.
- Bake the fish on the bottom rack in the oven for 15 to 20 minutes at 400°F or until the fish turns golden brown.
- Leave to rest for 10 minutes before serving.

2.21 Chicken with Mustard Sauce

Preparation time: 20 mins

Servings: 4

Ingredients

- 2 pounds boneless and skinless chicken, thinly sliced
- 1/4 cup shallots, diced
- 1/4 cup freshly chopped scallions
- 1/2 cup flour
- 3 tbsps. cup canola oil
- 2 cups low-sodium chicken stock
- 1 tbsp. low-sodium bouillon chicken base
- 2 tbsps. brown mustard
- 1/2 stick chilled, cubed unsalted butter

Seasonings

- 1/2 tsp. black pepper
- 1/2 tsp. Italian seasoning
- 1 tbsp. dried parsley
- 1 tbsp. smoked paprika

Nutritional facts per serving

- Calories: 336cal
- Fat: 13g
- Sodium: 124mg
- Protein: 25g
- Potassium: 432mg

- Phosphorus: 256mg
- Carbohydrates: 30g

Steps

- In a small container, mix the pepper, Italian seasoning, paprika, and parsley together.
- Sprinkle part of it on the chicken breast and add the remainder to the flour.
- Heat some the oil over medium-high heat in a large skillet.
- Place the chicken in the seasoned flour, drain the excess flour and set it aside.
- Sauté the chicken in the pan on both sides for two to three minutes.
- Remove the chicken and put it aside to rest. Add the shallots and sauté them until they are mildly translucent.
- Whisk in the leftover flour and continue to add stock steadily while continuing to whisk. Lower the heat and whisk in mustard, chicken bouillon, and unsalted butter after five minutes of cooking over medium-high heat.
- Turn the heat off and return the chicken and all the juice drippings back to the pan. Stir the food and serve with scallions.

2.22 Easy Mama's Meatloaf

Preparation time: 30 mins

Servings: 4

Ingredients

- 1 lb. lean minced beef or turkey
- 1 egg, beaten
- 1/2 cup breadcrumbs
- 2 tbsps. Mayonnaise

Seasonings

- 1 tsp. garlic powder
- 1 tsp. onion powder
- 1 tsp. low-sodium bouillon beef base

- 1 tbsp. low-sodium Worcestershire sauce
- 1/2 tsp. red pepper flakes

Nutritional facts per serving

- Calories: 368cal
- Fat: 24g
- Sodium: 332mg
- Protein: 26g
- Potassium: 461mg
- Phosphorus: 274mg
- Carbohydrates: 15g

Steps

- Preheat the oven to 375°F.
- In a medium-sized dish, mix all items together and stir thoroughly.
- Place the mixture in a meatloaf pan or shape it into an 8x4" oblong loaf and place it on a wide baking sheet tray.
- Cover and bake with aluminum foil for 20 minutes. Then, cut the foil and cook for an extra five minutes. Switch off the oven and leave the meat to rest in the oven before removing and serving after 10 minutes.

2.23 Spicy Grilled Pork Chops with Peach Glaze

Preparation time: 20 mins

Servings: 8

Ingredients

- 8 pork chops
- 1 cup peach preserves
- 2 tbsps. cilantro
- 1/4 cup lime juice
- Zest of 1 lime
- 1 tbsp. low-sodium soy sauce
- 1 tsp. smoked paprika
- 2 tsps. dried onion flakes
- 1/2 tsp. red pepper flakes
- 1/2 tsp. black pepper
- 1/4 cup olive oil

Nutritional facts per serving

- Calories: 358cal
- Fat: 19g
- Sodium: 159mg
- Protein: 24g
- Potassium: 364mg
- Phosphorus: 189mg
- Carbohydrates: 28g

Steps

- Turn the heat on.
- In a small bowl, combine all the ingredients together (except the pork chops).
- Take a quarter of the mixture and set it aside.
- Place the remaining marinade and the pork chops in a storage bag and marinate for four hours (overnight is even better).
- Grill the pork chops on each side for six to eight minutes.
- Glaze the meat one more time with the leftover marinade before removing the grill and allow them to rest for seven to ten minutes before serving.

2.24 Chicken & Gnocchi Stew

Preparation time: 20 mins

Servings: 10

Ingredients

- 2 lb. cubed chicken breast
- 1 lb. gnocchi
- 1/4 cup grape seed or light olive oil
- 1 tbsp. low-sodium bouillon chicken base
- 6 cups low-sodium chicken stock
- 1/2 cup celery, chopped
- 1/2 cup onions, chopped
- 1/2 cup carrots, chopped
- 1/4 cup parsley, chopped
- 1 tsp. black pepper
- 1 tsp. sodium free italian seasoning

Nutritional facts per serving

- Calories: 363cal
- Fat: 11g
- Sodium: 122mg
- Protein: 29g
- Potassium: 486mg
- Phosphorus: 296mg
- Carbohydrates: 39g

Steps

- Put the stockpot on the burner and add the oil.
- Put the chicken in the stockpot and allow it to sauté for a few minutes until it is golden brown.
- Add the celery, carrots, and onions and cook until they are translucent. Add the chicken stock and let it cook for 20 to 30 minutes on high heat.
- Add the chicken bouillon, black pepper, and Italian seasoning and reduce the heat, stirring occasionally.

- Add the gnocchi and simmer for 15 minutes, stirring continuously.
- Turn off the heat, add parsley and serve.

2.25 Bourbon Glazed Skirt Steak

Preparation time: 20 mins

Servings: 8

Ingredients

Bourbon glaze

- 1/4 cup shallots, diced
- 3 tbsps. unsalted, chilled butter
- 1 cup bourbon
- 1/4 cup dark brown sugar
- 2 tbsps. french mustard
- 1 tbsp. black pepper

Skirt steak

- 2 tbsps. grape seed oil
- 1/2 tsp. dried oregano
- 1/2 tsp. (smoked) paprika
- 1 tsp. black pepper
- 1 tbsp. (red wine) vinegar
- 2 lb. skirt steak

Nutritional facts per serving

- Calories: 410cal
- Fat: 23g
- Sodium: 152mg
- Protein: 25g
- Potassium: 284mg
- Phosphorus: 172mg
- Carbohydrates: 9g

Steps

Bourbon glaze

- Over a medium-high flame, sauté the shallots in one tablespoon of butter in a shallow saucepan.

- Reduce the heat, remove the pan from the burner, add the liquor, and return the saucepan to the burner.
- Cook for about 10 to 15 minutes or until around one-third of the sauce has evaporated.
- Place the brown sugar, mustard, and black pepper in the sauce and whisk briefly.
- Switch off the heat and whisk in the remaining two teaspoons of cold, cubed butter, stirring until everything is mixed well.

Skirt steak

- In a gallon-sized sealable storage container, combine the first 5 ingredients, add the steaks, and shake well.
- Enable the steaks to be marinated for 30 to 45 minutes at room temperature.
- Remove the steaks from the container, grill each side for 15 to 20 minutes.
- Brush the steaks with the glaze and grill them for four to six minutes more or until needed.
- Slice and serve the steaks

2.26 Chicken Pot Pie Stew

Preparation time: 1 hour

Servings: 8

Ingredients

- 1 1/2 lbs. fresh skinless, boneless chicken breast
- 2 cups low-sodium chicken stock
- 1/4 cup olive oil
- 1/2 cup flour
- 1/2 cup carrot, diced
- 1/2 cup onions, diced
- 1/4 cup celery, diced
- 1/2 tsp. black pepper
- 1 tbsp. (sodium-free) italian seasoning

- 2 tsps. low-sodium bouillon chicken base
- 1/2 cup frozen or fresh sweet peas
- 1/2 cup heavy cream
- 1 cooked piecrust, broken into bitesize pieces
- 1 cup cheddar cheese

Nutritional facts per serving

- Calories: 389cal
- Fat: 21g
- Sodium: 425mg
- Protein: 27g
- Potassium: 210mg
- Phosphorus: 291mg
- Carbohydrates: 23g

Steps

- Cut the chicken into small cubes.
- Put the chicken and stock in a wide stockpot and cook for 30 minutes on medium-high heat. Then, mix the oil and flour together.
- Add the oil and flour mixture to the chicken broth and whisk until it somewhat thickens. Reduce the heat and allow the food to simmer for 15 minutes.
- Add the carrots, onions, celery, black pepper, bouillon, and Italian seasoning to the broth and let it cook for an extra 15 minutes.
- Switch the heat off and add the peas and cream. Stir until everything is well balanced. Serve in mugs and top as a garnish with small quantities of cheese and piecrust.

2.27 Sauceless BBQ Baby Back Ribs

Preparation time: 1 hour

Servings: 8

Ingredients

- 2 slabs of baby back ribs
- 1 cup brown sugar
- 1 tsp. black pepper
- 1 tsp. red pepper flakes

- 1 tsp. smoked paprika
- 2 tsps. garlic powder
- 2 tsps. dehydrated onion flakes
- 2 tsps. dark chili powder

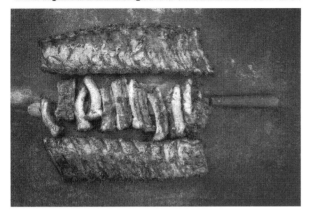

Nutritional facts per serving

- Calories: 324cal
- Fat: 16g
- Sodium: 102mg
- Protein: 19g
- Potassium: 453mg
- Phosphorus: 199mg
- Carbohydrates: 34g

Steps

- Preheat the oven to 400°F.
- Mix the rub ingredients in a small cup and slather the rub onto the ribs.
- Place the ribs in a rack-lined wire tray. Then, cover with aluminum foil securely and roast for up to two hours.
- Take the rack out of the oven, remove the ribs using a pair of tongs and put them on a plate.
- Turn the broiler on and cook the ribs under the broiler for 15 minutes or until the desired level of crispiness is achieved.
- Leave the ribs to rest for 5 to 10 minutes before cutting and eating.

2.28 Pork Loin with Sweet & Tart Apple Stuffing

Preparation time: 1 hour

Servings: 6

Ingredients

Cherry marmalade glaze

- 1/2 cup sugar-free orange marmalade
- 1/4 cup apple juice
- 1/2 cup ground dried cherries
- 1/8 tsp. cinnamon
- 1/8 tsp. nutmeg

Apple stuffing

- 2 tbsps. olive oil
- 2 cups cubed white bread
- 1/2 cup red apples, diced
- 2 tbsps. unsalted butter
- 2 tbsps. onions, chopped
- 2 tbsps. celery, chopped
- 1 tbsp. fresh thyme
- 1 tsp. black pepper
- 1/2 cup of low-sodium chicken stock

Roast pork loin

- 1 lb. boneless pork loin
- 2 18"-long pieces of butcher twine

Nutritional facts per serving

- Calories: 264cal
- Fat: 15g
- Sodium: 138mg
- Protein: 15g
- Potassium: 275mg
- Phosphorus: 154mg
- Carbohydrates: 22g

Steps

- Preheat the oven to 400°F.

- Sauté all the stuffing ingredients in olive oil in a broad pan over medium-high heat for two to three minutes, with the exception of chicken stock.
- Add the chicken stock to the pan slowly. It is not necessary to add all the stock as this depends on how much juice is released from the apples while they are frying.
- Remove the stuffing from the heat and let it rest until it reaches room temperature, before refrigerating.
- Meanwhile, cut five slits across the length of the meat, forming several pockets.
- Fill each pocket with about two teaspoons of stuffing.
- Hold the stuffing in place, tie one long piece of twine across the loin's length and add additional twine around the shorter length as needed.
- On a baking sheet plate, place the remaining stuffing and add on top of it the bound, stuffed pork loin.
- Bake the meat at 400°F for 45 minutes or until the internal temperature reaches 160°F.
- Combine all the glaze ingredients. Spoon the onto the meat, shut the oven off, and let the meat rest in the oven for 10 to 15 minutes. Remove the pork loin, slice it into sections, and then serve.

2.29 Spaghetti & Asparagus Carbonara

Preparation time: 15 min

Servings: 6

Ingredients

- 2 tsps. canola oil
- 1 cup onions, finely chopped
- 1 large egg, beaten
- 1 cup heavy cream
- 1/4 cup of salt-free chicken stock
- 3 cups spiral noodle pasta, cooked al dente (about 1.5 cups uncooked)
- 2 cups asparagus, chopped into 1"-long pieces
- 1 tsp. coarse black pepper
- 1/2 cup scallions, freshly chopped
- 3 tbsps. bacon bits
- 3 tbsps. shredded parmesan cheese

Nutritional facts per serving

- Calories: 255cal
- Fat: 13g
- Sodium: 160mg
- Protein: 10g
- Potassium: 303mg
- Phosphorus: 157mg
- Carbohydrates: 28g

Steps

- Heat the oil and sauté the onions in a large nonstick pan over medium-high heat until slightly browned.
- Meanwhile, mix the egg and the cream in a small bowl until they are completely combined.
- Lower the heat to mild and add the cream mixture onto the onions, stirring continuously for around four to six minutes with a wooden spoon before the mixture begins to thicken.
- Add the stock, pasta, asparagus, and black pepper and mix for another three to four minutes or until the stock warms up.
- Switch off the fire and pour the carbonara into a serving dish. Cover with scallions, cheese, and bacon bits. Serve while hot.

2.30 Zucchini Sauté

Preparation time: 15 min

Servings: 6

Ingredients

- 4 cups zucchini, sliced
- 1 cup whole milk
- 1/2 cup flour
- 1/4 cup shredded parmesan cheese
- 1/2 tsp. fresh basil
- 1/2 tsp. fresh thyme
- 1/2 tsp. fresh tarragon
- 2 tbsps. vegetable oil
- Pepper

Nutritional facts per serving

- Calories: 122cal
- Fat: 7g
- Sodium: 76mg
- Protein: 4g
- Potassium: 375mg
- Phosphorus: 92mg
- Carbohydrates: 13g

Steps

- Soak the zucchini in the milk.
- In a cup, mix the flour, parmesan cheese, pepper, and herbs.
- In a wide skillet, heat the vegetable oil.
- Dip the zucchini into a blend of cheese and herbs.
- Sauté the zucchini, serve, and enjoy.

2.31 Smothered Chops and Sautéed Vegetables

Preparation time: 1 hour

Servings: 6

Ingredients

Smothered pork chops

- 6 pork loin chops, bone-in
- 1 tbsp. black pepper
- 2 tsps. smoked paprika
- 2 tsps. ground onion powder
- 2 tsps. ground garlic powder
- 1 cup and 2 tbsps. flour
- 1/2 cup olive oil
- 2 cups low-sodium beef stock
- 1 1/2 cups onion, diced
- 1/2 cup scallions, freshly sliced

Sautéed greens

- 8 cups collard greens, chopped
- 2 tbsps. olive oil
- 1 tbsp. unsalted butter
- 1/4 cup onions, finely chopped
- 1 tbsp. garlic, diced
- 1 tsp. crushed red pepper flakes
- 1 tsp. black pepper
- 1 tsp. vinegar (optional)

Nutritional facts per serving

- Calories: 464cal
- Fat: 28g
- Sodium: 108mg
- Protein: 28g
- Potassium: 605mg
- Phosphorus: 289mg
- Carbohydrates: 27g

Steps

Pork chops

- Preheat the oven to 350°F.
- In a small container, mix the black pepper, paprika, ground onion, and garlic powder. Season the pork chops with half of the seasoning and mix the other half with one cup of flour.
- Coat the pork chops lightly with the seasoned flour.
- Heat some oil in a big Dutch oven or an oven-safe pot (without rubber handles).
- Fry the pork chops on each side for two to four minutes or until the desired level of crispness is achieved. Remove them from

the pot and dump all but two teaspoons of oil out.

- Cook the onions for around four to six minutes until they become translucent. Stir in two teaspoons of the reserved flour and mix them with the onions for around one minute.
- Add the beef stock and mix until it thickens.
- Place the pork chops back in the pot and coat them with sauce. Cover or seal with foil and bake in the oven at 350°F for at least 30 to 45 minutes.
- Remove the dish from the oven and leave it to rest for up to 10 minutes before serving.

Sautéed greens

- Blanch the greens in a pot of boiling water for 30 seconds.
- Strain the greens and move them to a bowl of chilled water.
- Allow the greens to cool, then strain, dry, and set them aside.
- Melt the butter and oil together in a wide saucepan over a medium-high flame. Add the onions and garlic and simmer for around four to six minutes until they brown.
- Add the collard greens and the black and red pepper and allow them to simmer on high heat for five to eight minutes, stirring continuously.
- Remove them from the heat. If necessary, add vinegar and stir.

CHAPTER 3. SALADS AND SALAD DRESSINGS

3.1 Polynesian Rice Salad

Preparation time: 20 mins

Servings: 12

Ingredients

- 1 cup corn oil
- 1/2 cup vinegar (balsamic)
- 1 3/4 tsps. black pepper
- 3 garlic cloves
- 1/2 tsp. dried basil
- 1/2 tsp. dried oregano
- 1/2 cup fresh parsley
- 2 cups chopped tomatoes
- 1/2 cup red onion, sliced
- 1 cup frozen artichoke hearts
- 1/3 cup fresh dill
- 6 cups cooked white rice
- 1 lb. cooked prawns
- 1/2 cup dried cranberries
- 1 cup (canned) pineapple chunks
- 1 cup frozen green peas

Nutritional facts per serving

- Calories: 251cal
- Fat: 15g
- Sodium: 160mg
- Protein: 9g
- Potassium: 182mg
- Phosphorus: 77mg
- Carbohydrates: 24g

Steps

- Mix the pepper, salt, minced garlic, vinegar, minced parsley, oregano, basil, with the oil and vinegar. Set the mixture aside.
- Chop the onion and pepper.
- Boil the artichoke hearts and the green peas.
- Combine the tomatoes, onion, rice, artichoke hearts, shrimps, pineapple, dill, peas, and cranberries in a large container.
- Stir the dressing into the salad and serve.

3.2 No Salt Pesto

Preparation time: 5 mins

Servings: 4

Ingredients

- 4 tbsps. pine nuts
- 2 fresh garlic cloves
- 1 1/2 olive oil
- 1 bunch fresh basil leaves
- Juice of 1/2 a lime
- Black pepper

Nutritional facts per serving

- Calories: 95cal
- Fat: 10g
- Sodium: 65mg
- Protein: 1g
- Potassium: 40mg
- Phosphorus: 16mg
- Carbohydrates: 1g

Steps

- Put the olive oil, nuts, and garlic in a blender or food processor and pulse for a few seconds.
- Then, add the black pepper, basil leaves, and lime juice and proceed to blend until a dense, smooth paste is made. Add more lime juice and black pepper to taste.
- The mixture is then ready for usage. If you apply a thin coat of olive oil on top, it lasts

for three to four days in the fridge. In ice cube trays, you can even freeze it and have convenient parts at any moment on standby.

3.3 Basil-Lime Pineapple Fruit Salad

Preparation time: 5 mins

Servings: 10

Ingredients

- 2 lbs. fresh pineapple chunks
- 1 lb. fresh strawberries
- 1 lb. fresh blueberries
- ½ cup granulated sugar
- 10g basil leaves
- Zest of 1 lime

Nutritional facts per serving

- Calories: 55cal
- Fat: 1g
- Sodium: 3mg
- Protein: 2g
- Potassium: 149mg
- Phosphorus: 19mg
- Carbohydrates: 13g

Steps

- Mix the pineapple with the sliced strawberries and blueberries.
- Place the sugar in a saucepan with ½ cup of water, turn on the heat and stir until dissolved.
- Turn off the heat, add the basil and lime zest and let cool
- In a large bowl mix the pineapple, strawberries, and blueberries with the syrup. Chill before serving.

3.4 Chicken Apple Crunchy Salad

Preparation time: 5 mins

Servings: 4

Ingredients

- 4 chicken breasts, cooked (about 1 lb.)
- 1 large size gala apple
- 1/2 cup chopped celery
- 2 tbsps. chopped spring onions
- 2 tbsps. dried dark raisins or cranberries
- 4 tbsps. low-fat mayonnaise
- 1 tbsp. low-fat sour cream
- 1 tbsp. lime juice
- 1/4 tsp. cinnamon
- 1/4 tsp. black pepper

Nutritional facts per serving

- Calories: 245cal
- Fat: 13g
- Sodium: 222mg
- Protein: 22g
- Potassium: 351mg
- Phosphorus: 159mg
- Carbohydrates: 14g

Steps

- Dice the celery, apples, and onions.
- In a large bowl, mix the celery, chicken, raisins, apples, and spring onions together.
- Combine the black pepper, lime juice, whipped cream, mayonnaise, and cinnamon together.
- Add the dressing to the salad, toss thoroughly and serve.

3.5 Crunchy Couscous Salad

Preparation time: 30 mins

Servings: 6

Ingredients

- 1 medium-sized cucumber
- 1 red (sweet) pepper
- 1/2 sweet onion
- 2 tsps. black olives
- 2 tbsps. flat-leaf parsley, chopped
- 3 oz. uncooked couscous
- 1 cup of water
- 2 tbsp. olive oil
- 1 oz. vinegar
- 1 oz. feta cheese crumbled
- Black pepper
- Basil leaves

Nutritional facts per serving

- Calories: 130cal
- Fat: 7g
- Sodium: 168mg
- Protein: 4g
- Potassium: 110mg
- Phosphorus: 56mg
- Carbohydrates: 17g

Steps

- Slice the cucumbers thinly. Then, proceed to chop the onion, garlic, and peppers.

- Cook the couscous in boiling water, then drain and let cool
- Add the onion, cucumber, parsley, peppers, and olives to the couscous.
- To prepare the seasoning, mix together feta cheese, olive oil, salt, pepper, vinegar, and chopped basil.
- Mix the couscous salad and serve.

3.6 Curried Fruit & Chicken Salad

Preparation time: 5 mins

Servings: 8

Ingredients

- 4 boneless or skinless chicken
- breasts, cooked
- 1 celery stalk
- 1/2 cup chopped onions
- 1 medium-sized apple
- 1/2 cup seedless red grapes
- 1/2 cup seedless green grapes
- 1/2 cup water chestnuts
- 1 pinch of black pepper
- 1/2 tsp. curry powder
- 1 grated carrot
- 4 tbsps. Mayonnaise

Nutritional facts per serving

- Calories: 239cal
- Fat: 19g
- Sodium: 163mg
- Protein: 15g
- Potassium: 201mg
- Phosphorus: 116mg
- Carbohydrates: 7g

Steps

- Dice the chicken, apples, and celery. Proceed to drain and cut the water chestnuts.

- Combine the carrots, onions, celery, chicken, grapes, apple, water chestnuts, pepper, mayonnaise, and curry powder in a large salad bowl. Toss everything together. Instantly serve or chill for later use.

3.7 Tuna Past Salad

Preparation time: 10 mins

Servings: 4

Ingredients

- 2 cups cooked fusilli pasta
- 1 stalk of celery
- 1 red sweet pepper
- 2 ripe tomatoes
- 1 tbsp. spring onions
- 1 tbsp. lemon zest
- 2 oz. low-fat mayonnaise
- 2 oz. low-sodium Italian seasoning for salads (next recipe)
- 1 low-sodium, tuna can

Nutritional facts per serving

- Calories: 267cal
- Fat: 15g
- Sodium: 137mg
- Protein: 14g
- Potassium: 150mg
- Phosphorus: 104mg

- Carbohydrates: 22g

Steps

- Chop the celery, spring onions, tomatoes, and pepper. In a mixing bowl, combine the cooked pasta with the vegetables and the drained tuna.
- Whisk the salad dressing, lemon zest and mayonnaise together in a separate bowl and pour the dressing over the salad.
- To allow the flavors to mix thoroughly, refrigerate for one hour.

3.8 Italian Dressing

Preparation time: 5 mins

Servings: 16

Ingredients

- 1 tbsp. dried parsley
- 1/4 tsp. ground oregano
- 1/2 tsp. ground thyme
- 1/4 tsp. ground marjoram
- 1/2 tsp. ground celery seeds
- 1/4 tsp. garlic powder
- 1 tsp. granulated sugar
- 1 pinch black pepper
- 1/2 cup vinegar
- 1/2 cup olive oil

Nutritional facts per serving

- Calories: 66cal
- Fat: 9g
- Sodium: 19mg
- Protein: 1g
- Potassium: 11mg
- Phosphorus: 2mg
- Carbohydrates: 1g

Steps

- Mix the seasonings, vinegar, and oil together. Shake well to mix.

3.9 Flowers & Greens Salad

Preparation time: 5 mins

Servings: 4

Ingredients

- 4 spring onions
- 1 small-sized cucumber
- 1 cup snap peas
- 1 small-sized pear
- 3 oz. feta cheese
- 1 oz. edible flowers
- 2 tbsps. yogurt
- 2 tbsps. Pomegranate syrup
- 1 tbsp white vinegar
- 2 tbsps. chopped dill
- 4 tbsps. olive oil
- 1 tsp. mustard

Nutritional facts per serving

- Calories: 213cal
- Fat: 11g
- Sodium: 128mg
- Protein: 12g
- Potassium: 218mg
- Phosphorus: 164mg
- Carbohydrates: 12g

Steps

- Chop the spring onions and thinly slice the cucumber.
- Slice the snap peas, core and slice the pear. Mix all the vegetables in a bowl.
- Crumble the feta cheese with a fork.
- Mix the yogurt, lemon juice, syrup, olive oil, mustard, and dill together in a mixer.
- Toss the salad with the dressing.
- Scatter some festa cheese on the salad. Add the edible flowers on top and serve.

3.10 Thai Salad with Corn

Preparation time: 5 mins

Servings: 6

Ingredients

- Zest of 2 limes
- Juice of 1 lime
- 2 garlic cloves, minced
- 2 to tbsps. sweet chili sauce
- 1/2 cup sweet corn
- 1/2 red onion, finely chopped
- 1/2 cup coriander, minced
- 1/2 cabbage shredded
- 1/2 cup of carrots, shredded

Nutritional facts per serving

- Calories: 62cal
- Fat: 9g
- Sodium: 85mg
- Protein: 3g
- Potassium: 163mg
- Phosphorus: 15mg
- Carbohydrates: 15g

Steps

- In a small cup, mix the garlic, sweet chili sauce, lime juice, and zest together. Mix them together until everything is well blended and set it aside.
- Mix the remaining ingredients in a wide bowl and toss them until they are well combined.
- Serve immediately or within the next 24 hours.

3.11 Tabbouleh

Preparation time: 35 mins

Servings: 8

Ingredients

- 1 cup bulgur wheat
- 1 cup hot water
- 1 diced and tomato
- 1/2 medium-sized, seeded, and diced cucumber
- 1/2 cup chopped parsley
- 2 tbsps. green onion, thinly sliced
- 1 tbsp. chopped fresh mint
- 1 pinch of pepper
- 3 tbsps. olive oil
- 3 tbsps. lime juice

Nutritional facts per serving

- Calories: 115cal
- Fat: 6g
- Sodium: 8mg
- Protein: 4g
- Potassium: 181mg
- Phosphorus: 67mg
- Carbohydrates: 16g

Steps

- Pour the hot water into the bowl with the bulgur and let stand for 30 minutes.

- Mix the cucumber, tomato, parsley, mint, and green onion.
- Whisk the olive oil and lime juice with the pepper.
- Mix the cooked bulgur with the vegetables, add the dressing and mix well.
- Chill and serve.

3.12 Summer Salad

Preparation time: 5 mins

Servings: 4

Ingredients

- 1 lettuce head
- 8 strawberries, sliced
- 1 small red onion, chopped
- 1/4 cup slivered almonds, toasted
- 1 can mandarins, drained
- 1/4 cup olive oil
- 2 tbsps. (balsamic) vinegar
- 1 tsp. sugar
- 1 pinch of pepper

Nutritional facts per serving

- Calories: 251cal
- Fat: 3g
- Sodium: 96mg
- Protein: 6g
- Potassium: 266mg
- Phosphorus: 105mg
- Carbohydrates: 15g

Steps

- Combine the ingredients for the salad in a large salad dish.
- Place the sugar, olive oil, and balsamic vinegar in a jar and shake it to ensure everything is well blended.
- Add the dressing to the salad and toss.
- Serve and enjoy.

13. Raspberry Vinaigrette

Preparation time: 5 mins

Servings: 6

Ingredients

- 1/2 cup raspberry vinegar
- 1/4 cup oil
- 1 tsp. french mustard
- 1 tbsp. sugar
- 1/4 cup mint leaves, sliced

Nutritional facts per serving

- Calories: 95cal
- Fat: 10g
- Sodium: 22mg
- Protein: 1g
- Potassium: 15mg
- Phosphorus: 3mg
- Carbohydrates: 4g

Steps

- In a small container, mix all the ingredients at once.
- Use as a salad dressing.

3.14 Pomegranate & Persimmon Salad

Preparation time: 5 mins

Servings: 12

Ingredients

- 6 cups of chopped lettuce
- 1/2 cup pomegranate seeds
- 1/2 cup cashews or pecans, sliced
- 2 tsps. basil leaves
- 1/4 cup raspberry vinegar
- 2 tbsps. olive oil
- 2 or 3 fresh persimmons
- 8 oz. crumbled feta cheese

Nutritional facts per serving

- Calories: 135cal
- Fat: 9g
- Sodium: 106mg
- Protein: 6g
- Potassium: 87mg
- Phosphorus: 69mg
- Carbohydrates: 10g

Steps

- Place the lettuce in a serving bowl.
- Mix the vinegar, basil, pomegranate seeds, oil, and almonds together.
- Add the dressing and mix thoroughly.
- Peel and chop the persimmons and place them on top of the lettuce, along with the crumbled feta cheese.
- Refrigerate and serve.

3.15 Pasta Salad with Roasted Red Pepper Sauce

Preparation time: 20 mins

Servings: 8

Ingredients

- 2 tbsps. mayonnaise
- 8 fresh basil leaves
- 1 garlic clove
- 2 tbsps. vinegar (balsamic)

- 2 canned roasted bell peppers
- 16 oz. penne pasta
- 1 tbsp. olive oil
- 1 large-sized yellow onion, diced

Nutritional facts per serving

- Calories: 266cal
- Fat: 6g
- Sodium: 86mg
- Protein: 9g
- Potassium: 151mg
- Phosphorus: 92mg
- Carbohydrates: 48g

Steps

- In a food processor or mixer, mix the garlic, vinegar, peppers, mayonnaise, and basil together.
- Cook the pasta according to the package's instructions. Then, drain it and rinse with cold water before setting it aside.
- Heat the oil over low heat in a medium-sized frying pan.
- Add the onion and sauté until it is caramelized and softened.
- In a large bowl, mix the penne, caramelized onions, and sauce together.
- Serve immediately or store in the refrigerator.

3.16 Exotic Mango Salad

Preparation time: 5 mins

Servings: 4

Ingredients

- 2 large-sized mangos, diced
- 2 red peppers, diced
- 3 tbsps. lemon juice
- 2 tsps. honey
- 4 tbsps. fresh, minced coriander

1 hot pepper, finely chopped

Nutritional facts per serving

- Calories: 152cal
- Fat: 2g
- Sodium: 6mg
- Protein: 2g
- Potassium: 407mg
- Phosphorus: 39mg
- Carbohydrates: 39g

Steps

- Toss all the ingredients together and cool for one hour in the freezer.
- Serve when ready.

3.17 Beet Salad

Preparation time: 50 mins

Servings: 4

Ingredients

- 4 beets cooked in the oven for 40 minutes
- 1/2 cup cashews
- 4 crunchy lettuce leaves
- 2 tbsps. cup fresh basil, finely chopped
- 1/2 cup balsamic vinegar
- 1tsps sugar
- 1tbsps water
- 2 tsps. olive oil
- 3 oz. crumbled blue cheese

Nutritional facts per serving

- Calories: 284cal
- Fat: 21g
- Sodium: 242mg
- Protein: 7g
- Potassium: 394mg
- Phosphorus: 103mg
- Carbohydrates: 17g

Steps

- Peel the cooked roots and cut them into cubes.
- In a saucepan, add the cashews, water, and sugar. Heat the liquid, stirring continuously until caramelized.
- Place the cashews mixture on a parchment paper foil, let cool and then chop as desired.
- Whisk the dressing in a bowl; mix vinegar, oil, and basil, then add the beets and mix thoroughly.
- Use the lettuce leaves as a bed for the salad.
- Scatter the caramelized chopped pecans and the crumbled cheese over the top and serve.

3.18 Buttermilk & Herbs Dressing

Preparation time: 5 mins

Servings: 2

Ingredients

- 1/2 cup mayonnaise
- 1/2 cup buttermilk
- 2 tbsps. vinegar
- 1 tbsp. fresh minced chives
- 1 tbsp. of dill
- 1 tbsp. dried oregano
- 1 pinch garlic powder

Nutritional facts per serving

- Calories: 84cal
- Fat: 4g
- Sodium: 65mg
- Protein: 2g
- Potassium: 10mg
- Phosphorus: 1mg
- Carbohydrates: 2g

Steps

- Whisk the mayonnaise, buttermilk, and vinegar together in a medium-sized bowl.
- Add the chives, a pinch of garlic powder, oregano, and dill. Mix thoroughly.
- To help the flavors mix well together, chill the dressing for at least one hour.
- Stir well with the dressing before using on salads, meat, fish, vegetables.

3.19 Kicking Hot Coleslaw

Preparation time: 5 mins

Servings: 10

Ingredients

- 1 cup mayonnaise
- 1 tbsp. horseradish
- 2 tsps. apple cider vinegar
- 3 tbsps. granulated sugar
- 2 tsps. fresh dill, finely chopped
- 1 lb. mixed coleslaw with carrots

Nutritional facts per serving

- Calories: 108cal
- Fat: 4.5g
- Sodium: 171mg
- Protein: 1g
- Potassium: 118mg
- Phosphorus: 12mg

Carbohydrates: 9g

Steps

- Whisk together the horseradish, mayonnaise, sugar, dill, and vinegar in a large bowl.
- Chill the salad for at least one hour or overnight (preferably) before serving.

3.20 Peppers & Watermelon Salad

Preparation time: 5 mins

Servings: 6

Ingredients

- 3 cups seeded and diced watermelon
- 1 cup chopped green bell pepper
- 2 cups lemon juice
- 1 tbsp. coriander, minced
- 1 tbsp. spring onions, minced
- 2 medium jalapeños, chopped
- 1 garlic clove, minced

Nutritional facts per serving

- Calories: 31cal
- Fat: 0.4g
- Sodium: 3mg
- Protein: 2g
- Potassium: 129mg
- Phosphorus: 15mg
- Carbohydrates: 8g

Steps

- Mix all the ingredients together very well.
- Store the salad in the fridge for at least one hour.
- This salad is also perfect as a side for chicken or pork.

3.21 Crunchy Quinoa Salad

Preparation time: 15 mins

Servings: 8

Ingredients

- 1 cup rinsed quinoa
- 2 cups water
- 5 cherry tomatoes, chopped
- 1/2 cup cucumbers, chopped and seeded
- 3 green onions, chopped
- 4 tbsps. fresh mint, finely chopped
- 1/2 cup flat-leaf parsley, minced
- 2 tbsps. lemon juice
- 1 tbsp. grated lemon zest
- 4 tbsps. olive oil
- 4 tbsps. cup grated cheddar cheese
- 8 lettuce leaves

Nutritional facts per serving

- Calories: 159cal
- Fat: 10g
- Sodium: 47mg
- Protein: 6g
- Potassium: 238mg
- Phosphorus: 130mg
- Carbohydrates: 17g

Steps

- Rinse the quinoa until the water runs clear.
- Put the quinoa in a pan over medium heat with 1 tbsp. olive oil and sauté for two minutes, stirring continuously. Stir in two cups of water and bring it to a boil. Reduce the heat, cover the pan, and allow it to simmer for 10 minutes. Then, use a fork to fluff the quinoa.
- Combine the lime juice, mint, parsley, zest, and tomatoes with the olive oil, cucumbers, and onions. Add the cooled quinoa and mix again.
- Arrange the lettuce beds and divide the mixture between them. Scatter the cheese on top.

3.22 Lemon Orzo Spring Salad

Preparation time: 5 mins

Servings: 4

Ingredients

- 3/4 cup of orzo pasta
- 1/4 cup yellow pepper, cubed
- 1/4 cup red pepper, cubed
- 1/4 cup green pepper, cubed
- 1/2 cup of red spring onions,
- chopped
- 2 cups of zucchini, cubed
- 4 tbsps. olive oil
- 3 tbsps. fresh lime juice
- 1 tsp. lemon zest
- 3 tbsps. cheddar cheese, grated
- 2 tbsps. fresh rosemary, minced
- 1/2 tsp. black pepper
- 1/2 tsp. dried oregano
- 1/2 cup red pepper flakes

Nutritional facts per serving

- Calories: 331cal
- Fat: 23g
- Sodium: 80mg
- Protein: 7g
- Potassium: 377mg
- Phosphorus: 135mg
- Carbohydrates: 29g

Steps

- Cook the orzo pasta in accordance with the package directions and drain.
- In a wide pan over a medium-high flame, sauté the peppers, onions, and zucchini in two tbsps. of oil until they start to wilt.
- In a large bowl, whisk the lime juice, lime zest, 2 tbsps. of olive oil, cheese, rosemary, black pepper, red pepper flakes, and

oregano. Add the orzo pasta, sautéed vegetables and mix thoroughly once again.

- Allow it to cool at room temperature or serve immediately.

3.23 Cold Shrimps Noodle Salad

Preparation time: 5 mins

Servings: 10

Ingredients

- 1 lb. cooked and cooled pasta
- 4 cups of cooked shrimp
- 1 cup chopped scallions
- 2 cups cooked broccoli florets
- 1 cup chopped carrots
- 2 cups fresh, chopped shitake
- mushrooms
- 2 tbsps. sesame oil
- 2 tsps. chili oil
- 1/2 cup white rice vinegar
- 2 tbsps. chopped garlic
- 1 tbsp. fresh, chopped ginger
- 1/4 cup low-sodium soy sauce
- 1/4 cup fresh lemon juice
- 1 tbsp. lemon zest

Nutritional facts per serving

- Calories: 255cal
- Fat: 12g
- Sodium: 434mg
- Protein: 14g
- Potassium: 326mg
- Phosphorus: 230mg
- Carbohydrates: 28g

Steps

- Combine the pasta, shrimps, scallions, broccoli, mushrooms and carrots in a large salad bowl.

- Use a mixer to blend together the rest of the ingredients for around one minute.
- Add the pasta and vegetables mixture to the dressing mix, toss until it is well coated, and then serve immediately.

3.24 Pea Salad with Ginger-Lime Dressing

Preparation time: 10 mins

Servings: 6

Ingredients

- 1 cup sugar snap peas
- 1 cup snow peas
- 1 cup thawed, fresh sweet peas

Dressing

- 1 tsp. low-sodium soy sauce
- 1/4 cup fresh lemon juice
- 1 tsp. fresh lemon zest
- 2 tsps. fresh ginger fresh, chopped
- 1/2 cup olive oil
- 1 tbsp. hot sesame oil
- 1 tbsp. sesame seeds
- 1 pinch black pepper

Nutritional facts per serving

- Calories: 226cal
- Fat: 7g
- Sodium: 71mg
- Protein: 4g
- Potassium: 118mg
- Phosphorus: 41mg
- Carbohydrates: 7g

Steps

- In a hot skillet, gently toast the sesame seeds, flipping them continuously for around three to five minutes.
- Blanch all three types of peas for two minutes in a big pot of boiling water over high heat. Drain and then place in an iced water bowl. Stain when cooled.
- Mix the lemon juice and zest, black pepper, and soy sauce in a small bowl for around two minutes
- Continue whisking and add the ginger, olive oil and sesame oil.
- Combine the salad dressing with the pea mix in a large serving dish. Scatter the toasted sesame seeds on top and serve.

3.25 Shrimps & Couscous Salad

Preparation time: 15 mins

Servings: 4

Ingredients

- 1 1/2 cups of water
- 1 cup couscous, uncooked
- 1 lb. cooked shrimp
- 1 1/2 cups red pepper, chopped
- 1/4 cup green onions, diced
- 1/2 cup fresh basil, chopped
- 1/4 cup low-sodium chicken broth
- 3 tbsps. fresh lime juice
- 1 tbsp. olive oil

Nutritional facts per serving

- Calories: 341cal
- Fat: 9g
- Sodium: 811mg

- Protein: 27g
- Potassium: 376mg
- Phosphorus: 445mg
- Carbohydrates: 41g

Steps

- Cook the couscous in boiling water according to the package directions.
- Fluff with a fork and allow it to cool.
- In a large container, mix the seafood, couscous, basil, green onions, and peppers together.
- For the dressing, whisk in a small bowl the broth, lemon juice, and olive oil. Pour the dressing over the salad, toss gently and serve.

CHAPTER 4. SNACKS & BEVERAGES

4.1 Hot Turkey Wings

Preparation time: 50 mins

Servings: 7

Ingredients

- 7 whole turkey wings
- 2 tsps. hot chili powder
- 2 tsps. garlic powder
- 2 tsps. onion powder
- 1 1/2 cups reduced-sodium barbecue sauce
- 1 tsp. smoked paprika
- 1 tsp. red pepper flakes
- 1 tsp. black pepper
- 1 cup brown sugar

Nutritional facts per serving

- Calories: 273cal
- Fat: 3g
- Sodium: 372mg
- Protein: 20g
- Potassium: 322mg
- Phosphorus: 156mg
- Carbohydrates: 47g

Steps

- Preheat the oven to 375°F.
- Score the dried wings on both sides with a knife.
- Rub the wings with the spice rub, making them penetrate the slits.
- Place the wings on a baking tray, cover them, and bake for 30 minutes.
- Remove the foil, flip the wings, and cook for 30 minutes more.
- Let the wings rest for 15 minutes in the switched-off oven. Baste the wings with the low-sodium barbecue sauce and serve.

4.2 Chile Chipotle Wings

Preparation time: 30 mins

Servings: 4

Ingredients

- 1/4 cup honey
- 1/4 cup slightly soft butter
- 1 lb. jumbo chicken wings, divided
- 1 tbsp. green onions, chopped
- 1 tsp. black pepper
- 1 1/2 tbsp. chopped chipotle peppers in adobo sauce
- 1 tbsp. olive oil

Nutritional facts per serving

- Calories: 384cal
- Fat: 27g
- Sodium: 100mg
- Protein: 21g
- Potassium: 267mg
- Phosphorus: 147mg
- Carbohydrates: 19g

Steps

- Preheat the oven to 400°F.
- Place the divided chicken wings on a large nonstick baking tray. Add the olive oil and toss.
- Cook the wings on the oven for around 20 minutes, turning when they become crispy on one side.
- In a wide dish, combine the other ingredients and mix thoroughly until combined.
- Remove the wings from the oven and toss them in the seasoning until properly coated.
- Serve hot.

4.3 Cornbread Muffins & Lime Cardamom Butter

Preparation time: 40 mins

Servings: 12

Ingredients

- 3 tbsps. lime juice
- 2 tbsps. honey
- 1 tbsp. vanilla extract
- 1 1/2 stick soft butter
- 1 egg
- 1 cup milk
- 1 cup flour
- 1 cup cornmeal
- 1 1/2 tsp. baking soda
- 1/2 tsp. lime zest
- 1/2 tsp. orange extract
- 1/4 tsp. powdered cardamom

Nutritional facts per serving

- Calories: 209cal
- Fat: 14g
- Sodium: 180mg
- Protein: 4g
- Potassium: 88mg
- Phosphorus: 68mg
- Carbohydrates: 21g

Steps

- Preheat the oven to 350°F.
- Prepare the lime cardamom butter: in a bowl whisk 1 stick of softened butter, honey, lime zest, orange extract and cardamom until they are well combined.
- Mix the cornmeal, flour, and baking soda. In a separate bowl mix the egg, milk and 1/2 softened stick of butter, beating thoroughly.
- Then, proceed to fold the dried ingredients into the liquid ingredients making sure not to over mix.
- Coat the muffin tins with nonstick spray, and then proceed to fill each cup until it is three-quarters full. Bake the muffins for around 15/18 minutes.
- Serve the hot muffins with the lime cardamom butter.

4.4 Protein Chocolate Smoothie

Preparation time: 5 mins

Servings: 4

Ingredients

- 1 pinch of nutmeg
- 1 pinch of cinnamon
- 2 scoops of chocolate whey protein

- 2 cups ice
- 1/2 cup evaporated milk
- 1/4 cup condensed milk
- 2 tbsps. Chocolate liqueur (optional)

Nutritional facts per serving

- Calories: 143cal
- Fat: 5g
- Sodium: 134mg
- Protein: 11g
- Potassium: 248mg
- Phosphorus: 163mg
- Carbohydrates: 18g

Steps

- In a food processor, mix everything together (except for the cinnamon) for around two minutes.
- Serve in glasses and sprinkle with cinnamon as a garnish.

4.5 Buffalo Chicken Cucumber Salad

Preparation time: 40 mins

Servings: 8

Ingredients

- 4 tbsps. crumbled blue cheese
- 4 tbsps. chopped parsley
- 1/2 cup mayonnaise
- 1/2 tsp. black pepper
- 1/2 tsp. Italian seasoning
- 1 tbsp. chopped garlic
- 1 tsp. cayenne pepper
- 1 tsp. smoked paprika
- 2 large cucumbers
- 3 tbsps. fresh chives, chopped
- 2 tbsps. hot sauce
- 2 tbsps. lemon juice
- 3 cups shredded chicken breast

Nutritional facts per serving

- Calories: 156cal
- Fat: 14g
- Sodium: 253mg
- Protein: 19g
- Potassium: 284mg
- Phosphorus: 160mg
- Carbohydrates: 5g

Steps

- Scoop out the center of the cucumbers and discard. Cut in slices.
- In a bowl, mix all the ingredients together, except the cucumbers and chicken.
- Stir in the chicken and mix until it is well coated before refrigerating for about 30 minutes.
- Place the cucumber slices on a serving plate, pour the chicken mix over and garnish with parsley.

4.6 Crispy Cauliflower Phyllo Cups

Preparation time: 25 mins

Servings: 24

Ingredients

- 4 slices bacon
- 3 phyllo dough sheets
- 3 eggs
- 2 tbsps. chopped jalapeños
- 2 tbsps. butter
- 1 1/2 cups cooked cauliflower florets
- 1 tbsp. mint
- 1/2 tsp. hot pepper flakes
- 1/2 tsp. ground black pepper
- 1 cup shredded cheddar cheese
- 4 tbsps. cup spring onions, fincly diccd
- 1 pinch black pepper

Nutritional facts per serving

- Calories: 69cal
- Fat: 6g
- Sodium: 108mg
- Protein: 4g
- Potassium: 43mg
- Phosphorus: 50mg
- Carbohydrates: 3g

Steps

- Preheat the oven to 375°F.
- Scramble the eggs in a pan with 1 tbsp of olive oil. Remove and set aside.
- Melt the butter in the same pan. Sauté the diced bacon until crispy. Add the spring onions, onions, jalapeños, cauliflower, and hot pepper flakes and sauté until the onions becomes caramelized. Season with ground black pepper and mint.
- Add the cheese of the pan, turn the heat off and let cool.
- Take each phyllo sheet and cut them into 24 square-shaped pieces (total 72 pieces) and layer them 3 by 3 them into a mini muffin tin pan.
- Fill each muffin cup with equal quantities of the mixture and bake around 15 minutes or until the edges of the phyllo become slightly crispy. Take out of the oven, let cool for a couple of minutes and serve.

4.7 Cereal Protein Bars

Preparation time: 20 mins

Servings: 12

Ingredients

- 2 1/2 cups toasted rolled oats
- 1 cup dried cranberries
- 4 oz. crunchy peanut butter
- 4 oz. cup honey
- 4 oz. cup flaxseeds

- 4 oz. cup cashews

Nutritional facts per serving

- Calories: 284cal
- Fat: 14g
- Sodium: 50mg
- Protein: 8g
- Potassium: 259mg
- Phosphorus: 178mg
- Carbohydrates: 40g

Steps

- Toast the oats in a hot pan about 10 minutes at they turn golden brown.
- Mix all the ingredients together in a bowl.
- Put a sheet of parchment paper on a plate; pour the mix and try to shape a loaf. Wrap and then refrigerate for a minimum of one hour or overnight.
- Cut the protein bars into the desired shape and serve.

4.8 Homemade Savory Biscuits

Preparation time: 30 mins

Servings: 12

Ingredients

- 4 tbsps. cup mayonnaise
- 1/2 tsp baking soda
- 6 oz. cup skimmed milk
- 1 tsp. cream of tartar
- 1 3/4 cups all-purpose flour
- 1 tbsp. fresh chopped parsley
- 1 tbsp. fresh chopped rosemary
- 1 tbsp. fresh chopped chives
- Non-stick cooking spray

Nutritional facts per serving

- Calories: 110cal
- Fat: 5g
- Sodium: 89mg

- Protein: 4g
- Potassium: 86mg
- Phosphorus: 35mg
- Carbohydrates: 16g

Steps

- Preheat the oven to 350°F. Then, apply non-stick cooking spray to a baking sheet.
- Mix the flour, cream of tartar and baking soda in a bowl. Then, mix in the mayonnaise until the paste looks like coarse cornmeal.
- Add the milk and herbs to the flour mixture and mix well.
- Spoon the mix on the baking sheet and bake for about 12 minutes or until golden brown.
- Serve the biscuits immediately or refrigerate.

4.9 Angel's Deviled Eggs

Preparation time: 20 mins

Servings: 4

Ingredients

- 4 large eggs (hard-boiled and peeled)
- 2 tbsps. light mayonnaise
- 1 tbsp. onion, finely chopped
- 1/2 tsp. apple cider vinegar
- 1/2 tsp. dry mustard
- 1/2 tsp. ground black pepper

- 1 pinch of smoked paprika

Nutritional facts per serving

- Calories: 99cal
- Fat: 8g
- Sodium: 125mg
- Protein: 7g
- Potassium: 74mg
- Phosphorus: 91mg
- Carbohydrates: 3g

Steps

- Cut the eggs in half lengthwise. Spoon out the yolks and place the egg whites on a tray.
- Mash the yolks with a fork adding the dried mustard, onion, vinegar, mayonnaise and black pepper.
- Refill the half egg whites with the seasoned yolk mixture.
- Refrigerate and serve sprinkling with smoked paprika.

4.10 Beef Jerky

Preparation time: 40 mins

Servings: 30

Ingredients

- 1 1/2 tsps. Worcestershire sauce
- 1 tsp. garlic powder
- 1 tsp. hot pepper sauce
- 1/2 cup red dry wine
- 4 tbsps. dark brown sugar
- 2 tbsps. liquid smoke
- 1 tbsp. Tabasco sauce
- 3 lb. flank steak (or other lean meat)
- 1/2 cup low-sodium soy sauce

Nutritional facts per serving

- Calories: 101cal
- Fat: 8g
- Sodium: 101mg

- Protein: 13g
- Potassium: 102mg
- Phosphorus: 191mg
- Carbohydrates: 5g

Steps

- Trim or remove all the fat from the meat.
- Cut it lengthwise into 30 long strips along the grain.
- Place the strips in a mixing bowl.
- Whisk all the other ingredients together and pour them over the meat. Allow the meat to marinate for six hours or overnight in the refrigerator.
- Remove the meat from the marinade and pat dry with kitchen paper.
- If you have a dehydrator, dry out the meat for about 5 to 20 hours at 145°F.
- Otherwise, Preheat the oven to 175°F, place a baking sheet over the wire rack and distribute the meat, ensuring that the strips do not overlap.
- Bake the beef for 10 to 12 hours until it is very dry and brittle.

4.11 Edamame Guacamole

Preparation time: 20 mins

Servings: 6

Ingredients

- 3/4 cup frozen green soybeans or edamame (thawed)
- 3 tbsps. water
- 2 tbsps. olive oil
- 1/4 cup chopped parsley leaves
- 1 tbsp. lemon zest
- 1 tbsp. lemon juice
- 1 garlic clove
- 1/4 tsp. hot sauce

Nutritional facts per serving

- Calories: 75cal
- Fat: 2g
- Sodium: 6mg
- Protein: 4g
- Potassium: 143mg
- Phosphorus: 39mg
- Carbohydrates: 4g

Steps

- Put all the ingredients in a food processor and pulse until the mixture becomes smooth.
- Cover and refrigerate.
- Serve with tortilla chips or wedges of pita (next recipe).

4.12 Savory Pita Wedges

Preparation time: 15 mins

Servings: 8

Ingredients

- 1 tsp. dried rosemary
- 1/2 cup parmesan cheese, grated
- 4 rounds pita bread
- 4 tbsps. melted unsalted butter

Nutritional facts per serving

- Calories: 105cal
- Fat: 6g
- Sodium: 162mg
- Protein: 4g
- Potassium: 31mg
- Phosphorus: 46mg
- Carbohydrates: 12g

Steps

- Brush 1 tbsp. of butter each over the pita bread.

- Cut each bread into 8 pieces and sprinkle with rosemary and parmesan.
- Toast the bread in an oven at 450°F until the cheese melts, 3 to 5 minutes.
- You may serve the pita wedges with edamame guacamole (previous recipe).

4.13 Rosemary Sage Crackers

Preparation time: 25 mins

Servings: 12

Ingredients

- 3 tbsps. vegetable oil
- 2 tbsps. and 1/3 cup parmesan cheese, grated
- 1/3 cup buckwheat flour
- 1/2 cup water
- 1 tsp. garlic powder
- 1 tbsp. sage, finely chopped
- 1 tbsp. rosemary, finely chopped
- 1 tbsp. olive oil
- 1 1/4 cups all-purpose flour

Nutritional facts per serving

- Calories: 110cal
- Fat: 4g
- Sodium: 39mg
- Protein: 4g
- Potassium: 35mg
- Phosphorus: 44mg
- Carbohydrates: 14g

Steps

- Preheat the oven to 350°F.
- In a medium-sized dish, mix all-purpose flour, minced rosemary and sage, buckwheat flour, and two tablespoons of parmesan cheese.
- Make a well in the center of the flour mixture.

- Pour the water and 3 tbsps. of vegetable oil into the well and mix everything together.
- Knead the dough with a rolling pin until it is less than one-eighth of an inch thick.
- Put the dough on a baking sheet and cut through the dough to make one-inch-long squares.
- Brush each square the dough with 1 tbsp. olive oil.
- Sprinkle some garlic powder and parmesan cheese on top.
- Bake until the dough is crispy or light brown, around 15 to 20 minutes
- Divide the dough into individual crackers and serve

4.14 Rhubarb Cooler

Preparation time: 1 hour

Servings: 8

Ingredients

- 8 cups water
- 1/3 cup dark sugar
- Fresh mint leaves
- 1 lime cut in 8 wedges
- 8 chopped rhubarb stalks

Nutritional facts per serving

- Calories: 44cal
- Fat: 0g

- Sodium: 2mg
- Protein: 0g
- Potassium: 148mg
- Phosphorus: 8mg
- Carbohydrates: 12g

Steps

- Boil the stalks in the water for about 1 hour.
- Strain the liquid, add the sugar and stir thoroughly until dissolved.
- Let cool in the fridge.
- Put ice into tall glasses and pour the tea.
- Garnish with lime wedges, mint leaves and serve.

4.15 Rhubarb Lemonade Punch

Preparation time: 25 mins

Servings: 6

Ingredients

- 6 oz. frozen lemonade concentrate
- 5 tbsps. dark sugar
- 2 cups lemonade soda
- 3 cups of frozen rhubarb
- 3 cups water

Nutritional facts per serving

- Calories: 135cal
- Fat: 0g
- Sodium: 12mg
- Protein: 2g
- Potassium: 144mg
- Phosphorus: 17mg
- Carbohydrates: 35g

Steps

- In a pot mix all the ingredients, except the soda.
- Cover and simmer until the rhubarb becomes tender, around half an hour.

- Strain and let the liquid cool in the refrigerator
- Just before serving, put ice in tall glasses, pour the rhubarb mixture over the ice and top with chilled soda.

4.16 Hot Apple Punch

Preparation time: 15 mins

Servings: 8

Ingredients

- 2 quarts apple juice
- 1/2 tsp. cloves
- 2 cinnamon sticks
- 1 tsp. allspice
- 1 pinch nutmeg

Nutritional facts per serving

- Calories: 115cal
- Fat: 0g
- Sodium: 29mg
- Protein: 0g
- Potassium: 256mg
- Phosphorus: 2mg
- Carbohydrates: 29g

Steps

- Heat the apple over medium heat
- Add the remaining ingredients and bring the mixture to a simmer for around 10 minutes.
- Strain the cider into mugs and serve hot or pour into a thermos for later use.

4.17 Moose Jerky

Preparation time: 2 hours

Servings: 22

Ingredients

- 3 lbs. rump moose meat

- 2 tsps. liquid smoke
- 1/2 tsp. ground black pepper
- 1/2 tsp. powdered onion
- 1/2 tsp. powdered garlic
- 1/4 cup low-sodium soy sauce

Nutritional facts per serving

- Calories: 69cal
- Fat: 1g
- Sodium: 202mg
- Protein: 15g
- Potassium: 199mg
- Phosphorus: 103mg
- Carbohydrates: 1g

Steps

- Trim all the fat from the meat and cut into half-inch-thick strips.
- Whisk all the marinade ingredients in a bowl. Add the meat strips, mix well and let it marinate in the fridge for six hours.
- Proceed to preheat the oven to 180°F.
- Use parchment paper to cover a tray; spread the meat strips on the tray and cook for around two hours.
- Switch the heat off, let the meat cool in the oven and serve.

4.18 Baba Ghanouj

Preparation time: 30 mins

Servings: 8

Ingredients

- 8 large, unpeeled garlic cloves
- 1 large eggplant
- 2 tbsps. olive oil
- Lemon juice
- 1tbsp. chopped parsley
- 1/2 tsp. black ground pepper

Nutritional facts per serving

- Calories: 52cal
- Fat: 4g
- Sodium: 3mg
- Protein: 2g
- Potassium: 171mg
- Phosphorus: 23mg
- Carbohydrates: 6g

Steps

- Heat the oven to 350°F. Line a baking tray with parchment paper.
- Cut the eggplant in half and place the halves on the tray, cut side down.
- Cutoff the garlic cloves ends, place them on an aluminum foil, close the packet and put it on the baking tray.
- Roast the eggplant and garlic; after 20 minutes take the garlic packet out of the oven. Cook the eggplant until the flesh becomes very soft, around 40 more minutes.
- Turn the oven off, let the eggplant cool and remove the skin. Open the garlic packet and remove the garlic skin.
- Place the garlic, eggplant flesh, oil, lemon juice and parsley in a food processor. Pulse until smooth and season with ground black pepper.
- Serve with pita bread.

4.19 Spicy Eggplant Dip

Preparation time: 1 hour

Servings: 6

Ingredients

- 1 medium eggplant
- 1 tsp. olive oil
- 1 tbsp. lemon juice
- 1/4 cup fresh coriander
- 1/4 tsp. hot pepper flakes
- 1 tbsp. chopped garlic
- 1 tbsp. chopped green onions

Nutritional facts per serving

- Calories: 24cal
- Fat: 1g
- Sodium: 3mg
- Protein: 2g
- Potassium: 199mg
- Phosphorus: 24mg
- Carbohydrates: 6g

Steps

- Preheat the oven at 350°F
- Cut the eggplant in half, drizzle with olive oil. Roast the eggplant cut face down on a baking tray lined with parchment paper. When the eggplant is very tender, around 1 hour, turn the oven off.
- Let the eggplant cool and discard the skin.
- In a food processor, mix all the ingredients together until they become smooth.
- Serve with pita bread or crackers.

4.20 Spicy Crab Dip

Preparation time: 20 mins

Servings: 6

Ingredients

- 6 oz. crab meat
- 1 cup soft cream cheese
- 1 tbsp. spring onion, chopped
- 1 tsp. lemon juice
- 1 pinch ground black pepper
- 2 tbsps. cream
- 2 tsps. low-sodium soy sauce
- 1/2 tsp. hot pepper flakes

Nutritional facts per serving

- Calories: 99cal
- Fat: 10g
- Sodium: 133mg
- Protein: 6g
- Potassium: 92mg
- Phosphorus: 62mg
- Carbohydrates: 3g

Steps

- Preheat the oven to 375°F.
- In a bowl, mix with a spoon the cream cheese, spring onion, soy sauce, lemon juice, hot pepper, and black pepper. Add the cream, crab meat and mix thoroughly.
- Place the mixture in a baking dish and bake uncovered for around for 15 minutes, until the surface of the mix is sizzling. Serve with crackers or pita bread.

4.21 Crab Pies

Preparation time: 20 mins

Servings: 8

Ingredients

- 1 tbsps. olive oil
- 2 tbsps. parsley, chopped
- 4 tbsps. green onions, chopped
- 1 pinch ground black pepper
- 4 oz. crab meat
- 1/4 cup green peppers, diced
- 1/4 cup panko breadcrumbs
- 1 tsp. lemon juice
- 1 egg, beaten
- 1 garlic clove, chopped

Nutritional facts per serving

- Calories: 76cal
- Fat: 6g
- Sodium: 89mg
- Protein: 6g
- Potassium: 117mg
- Phosphorus: 61mg
- Carbohydrates: 5g

Steps

- Mix all the ingredients except the olive oil in a mixing bowl.
- Divide the mixture into eight equal parts.
- Shape the crab cakes by hand and place them on a tray.
- Heat the olive oil in a wide pan and fry the crab cakes on each side for about two minutes or until they are golden brown.
- Serve immediately.

CHAPTER 5. SOUPS & STEWS

5.1 Cauliflower & Pear Soup

Preparation time: 30 mins

Servings: 8

Ingredients

- 1 1/2 lb. cauliflower florets
- 2 pears, peeled cored and diced
- 3 apples, cored and diced
- 4 tbsps. honey
- 3 tbsps. olive oil
- 1 tbsp. chopped garlic
- 1 red onion, finely chopped
- 1 carrot, chopped
- 6 cups vegetable stock
- 2 tbsps. fresh ginger, chopped
- 2 tsps. ground cloves
- 8 toasted bread slices
- 1 tbsp. fresh thyme
- 2 tbsps. apple cider vinegar

Nutritional facts per serving

- Calories: 193cal
- Fat: 7g
- Sodium: 193mg
- Protein: 3g
- Potassium: 376mg
- Phosphorus: 52mg
- Carbohydrates: 37g

Steps

- Heat the oil to a wide pan and sauté the cauliflower florets, apples, onion, carrot and pears about 15 minutes, until softened.
- Add the garlic, ginger, apple cider vinegar, cloves, and vegetable stock. Bring it to a boil and simmer for around 15 minutes.
- Mash the soup by a hand blender.
- Serve with toasted bread and garnish with thyme.

5.2 Zucchini Curried Soup

Preparation time: 20 mins

Servings: 4

Ingredients

- 1 medium-sized onion, finely chopped
- 2 ground garlic cloves
- 2 cups low-sodium vegetable stock
- 2 cups oat milk
- 3 tbsps. oat flour
- 1 tsp. basil
- 1 tsp. curry powder
- 1/2 tsp. parsley
- 2 small-sized zucchinis, grated
- 1 medium-sized carrot, grated

Nutritional facts per serving

- Calories: 125cal
- Fat: 2g
- Sodium: 108mg
- Protein: 5g
- Potassium: 373mg
- Phosphorus: 137mg
- Carbohydrates: 25g

Steps

- Soften the garlic and onion in a pan with 2 tbsps. of water, on medium heat. Stir in the curry powder, milk and stock and bring to simmer.
- Whisk in the oatmeal, parsley and basil; add the grated carrots and zucchini.
- Lower the heat and wait for the vegetables to soften for about five minutes.
- Serve hot.

5.3 Old Fashioned Northern Stew

Preparation time: 8 hours

Servings: 8

Ingredients

- 1 lb. boneless beef
- 1 cup onion, finely chopped
- 6 garlic cloves, peeled
- 1 tbsp. of whole-grain mustard
- 2 cups of turnips, cubed
- 1 cup carrots, sliced
- 4 cups shredded broccoli florets
- 4 cups low-sodium beef stock
- 1 pinch black pepper
- 2 tbsps. chopped parsley

Nutritional facts per serving

- Calories: 186cal
- Fat: 10g
- Sodium: 154mg
- Protein: 18g
- Potassium: 543mg
- Phosphorus: 185mg
- Carbohydrates: 12g

Steps

- Trim all the fat from the meat and cube it. In hot pan, sauté the beef in the oil. Add the onion and garlic and sauté until softened.
- Setup the slow cooker; add the meat, onion and garlic with all their drippings, the beef stock and the mustard.
- Add all the remaining ingredients, cover and simmer for around eight hours on low or until the meat is tender.
- Add the black pepper and parsley and serve.

5.4 Persian Barley Soup

Preparation time: 2 hours

Servings: 8

Ingredients

- 4 pints of low-sodium vegetable stock
- 2 tbsps. olive oil
- 1 spring onion, finely chopped
- 1 cup barley, uncooked
- 1 tsp. turmeric
- Juice of 1 lime
- 4 tbsps. tomato paste
- 1 cup carrots, diced
- 1/2 cup greek yogurt
- 4 tbsps. parsley, chopped
- 1 lime divided in 8 wedges

Nutritional facts per serving

- Calories: 233cal
- Fat: 11g
- Sodium: 425mg
- Protein: 11g
- Potassium: 518mg
- Phosphorus: 126mg
- Carbohydrates: 27g

Steps

- Heat the vegetable stock in a small pot and bring it to simmer
- In a pot heat the olive oil over medium-high heat and sauté the onion until it is wilted. Add the barley stirring for one minute. Add the tomato paste, turmeric and pepper. Pour in the chicken stock, bring it to a boil and let the mixture simmer over low heat for one hour.
- Add the carrots and boil for 40 minutes or until the soup thickens and the carrots and barley are soft.
- Spoon the yogurt in a small container. Slowly add half a cup of the heated soup mixture to the yogurt while constantly whisking.
- Add the contents of the small container to the pot and keep whisking. Add the freshly chopped parsley and serve with fresh lime cut into wedges.

5.5 Mushroom & Kale Chicken Stew

Preparation time: 20 mins

Servings: 6

Ingredients

- 1/4 cup fresh onion, chopped
- 1 clove garlic, chopped
- 1/2 cup red pepper, chopped
- 1/2 cup shitake mushrooms, chopped
- 1/2 cup button mushrooms, chopped
- 1 cup kale, chopped
- 1 tbsp. olive oil
- 2 cups cooked, shredded turkey
- 2 cups low-sodium vegetable stock
- 1/2 tsp. smoked paprika
- 1/4 tsp. powdered garlic
- 1/2 tsp. ground black pepper
- 1 tbsp. cornstarch
- 1/2 cup milk

Nutritional facts per serving

- Calories: 200cal
- Fat: 7g
- Sodium: 95mg
- Protein: 26g
- Potassium: 501mg
- Phosphorus: 255mg
- Carbohydrates: 13g

Steps

- In a large frying pan, sauté the garlic and onion together until they start to wilt. Add all the veggies and stir fry until lightly brown.
- Add the turkey, spices, and vegetable stock and allow it to simmer gently.
- Whisk the cornstarch and milk together and add the mix to the simmering stew.
- Once the stew has thickened, it is ready to eat.
- Serve with rice or your favorite noodles.

5.6 Apple Cauliflower Soup with Garlic Croutons

Preparation time: 1 hour

Servings: 12

Ingredients

- 1 cauliflower, divided to small-sized florets
- 1 cup spring onion, chopped
- 2 red apples, diced
- 2 garlic cloves, chopped
- 1 tsp. rosemary
- 1 tsp. thyme
- 1 tsp. sage
- 1/2 teaspoon black pepper
- 1 1/2 quart of vegetable low-sodium stock

Nutritional facts per serving

- Calories: 83cal
- Fat: 2g
- Sodium: 125mg
- Protein: 4g
- Potassium: 231mg
- Phosphorus: 65mg
- Carbohydrates: 16g

Steps

- Heat the oven to 350°F.
- Wrap the peeled and oiled garlic cloves in aluminum foil; make a packet and cook in the oven for 30 minutes. Add the bread slices on a baking tray and toast for about 10.
- Take the garlic and bread out of the oven and let cool. Mash the garlic and spread over the bread slices.
- Place in a pot the onions, herbs, and vegetable stock. Bring a boil, then lower the heat and let it simmer for 30/35 minutes until the vegetables are softened to your taste.
- Blend the soup with a hand mixer until it is creamy.
- Pour into individual dishes, garnish the soup with a crouton and serve.

5.7 Jalapeño Chicken Stew

Preparation time: 30 mins

Servings: 4

Ingredients

- 1lb. boned chicken thighs
- 1 tbsp. olive oil
- 2 1/2 cups low-sodium vegetable stock
- 4 garlic cloves, minced
- 2 tbsps. chopped jalapeno
- 1 tbsp. all-purpose flour
- 1 red pepper, chopped
- 1 small-sized carrot, chopped
- 1 cup of corn
- 1/4 tbsp. ground black pepper
- 1/2 tsp. ground cumin
- 2 tsps. fresh coriander, minced
- 1 tbsp. cornstarch

Nutritional facts per serving

- Calories: 285cal
- Fat: 6g
- Sodium: 120mg
- Protein: 39g
- Potassium: 660mg
- Phosphorus: 359mg
- Carbohydrates: 24g

Steps

- Cut the chicken thighs into bite sized pieces. Heat the olive oil in a pot and cook the chicken until browned.
- Add the garlic, cumin and jalapenos and sauté over medium-high heat, stirring regularly for about two minutes. Stir in the flour, lower the heat, and stir for another two minutes. Gradually add the vegetable stock whisking well to dissolve the flour and bring to a boil.

- Add the carrots, cumin, red pepper, corn, and pepper. Lower the heat, cover the pot, and let simmer for around 20 minutes until the meat is fully cooked.
- Take a ladle of soup and pour into a small bowl; add the cornstarch and whisk to dissolve. Add the cornstarch mix to the soup and keep stirring until the soup thickens.
- Turn off the heat, pour the stew into individual dishes, garnish with the chopped coriander and serve.

5.8 Smoked Chicken & Rice Soup

Preparation time: 40 mins

Servings: 8

Ingredients

- 1 cup spring onion, diced
- 1 cup celery, chopped
- 1 cup carrot, diced
- 2 tbsps. olive oil
- 3/4 cup uncooked white rice
- 1 tsp. smoked paprika
- 4 tbsps. parsley, chopped
- 1 bay leaf
- 2 quarts low-sodium chicken stock
- 4 boneless chicken thighs, cut into bite sized chunks
- 2 tbsps. lemon juice

Nutritional facts per serving

- Calories: 161cal
- Fat: 4g
- Sodium: 222mg
- Protein: 15g
- Potassium: 252mg
- Phosphorus: 91mg
- Carbohydrates: 20g

Steps

- Stir fry the diced vegetables in olive oil in a large pan until lightly browned.
- Add the chicken and cook for about 10 minutes, then add the rice and continue cooking until the rice appears translucent.
- Add the stock, rice, bay leaf, and smoked paprika; bring the mixture to a boil and then reduce the flame. Allow the soup to simmer for 20 minutes.
- Turn off the heat, add the lime juice, the chopped parsley and serve.

5.9 Corn & Fennel Soup

Preparation time: 40 mins

Servings: 4

Ingredients

- 2 tsps. vegetable oil
- 2 lbs. corn
- 2 spring onions, chopped
- 1 celery stalk, chopped
- 4 garlic cloves, chopped
- 3 cups fennel, chopped
- Black pepper
- 4 tbsps. parsley, chopped
- 4 pints iced water

Nutritional facts per serving

- Calories: 113cal
- Fat: 4g
- Sodium: 17mg
- Protein: 4g
- Potassium: 299mg
- Phosphorus: 77mg
- Carbohydrates: 23g

Steps

- In a pot, stir fry the spring onions, corn, garlic, celery, and fennel in the olive oil.

- Add the cold water and bring the soup to a boil. Let simmer for 30/40 minutes.
- Turn off the heat, pour the soup into individual dishes, garnish with parsley and black pepper and serve.

5.10 Smoked Red Pepper Soup with Garlic Bread

Preparation time: 20 mins

Servings: 6

Ingredients

- 1 10 oz. can roasted red peppers, chopped
- 5 cups of water
- 2 spring onions, chopped
- 4 garlic cloves, chopped
- 1 tbsp. olive oil
- 6 tbsps. parsley, chopped
- 1 tsp. smoked paprika
- 1 tsp. Tabasco hot sauce (optional)

Nutritional facts per serving

- Calories: 193cal
- Fat: 13g
- Sodium: 160mg
- Protein: 4g
- Potassium: 369mg
- Phosphorus: 65mg
- Carbohydrates: 19g

Steps

- Preheat the oven at 350°F. Finely mince 2 cloves of garlic and mix with 4 tbsps. Olive oil. Brush the mixture on the bread slice
- Place the bread slices on a baking tray and bake them for around 8 minutes or they turn golden brown. Check carefully so as not to burn them.
- In a pot, stir fry the chopped 4 cloves of garlic, spring onion and smoked paprika in 1 tbsp of olive oil until they soften.
- Add the peppers, the water and bring to a boil. Simmer for around 10 minutes, turn off the heat and blend the soup with a hand mixer.
- Pour the soup into individual dishes, garnish with parsley, add drops of hot sauce if desired, and serve.

5.11 Thai Fish Soup

Preparation time: 30 mins

Servings: 12

Ingredients

- 5 cups boiled water
- 12 shrimps, deveined and shelled
- 1 cup spring onions, chopped
- 1 tbsp. minced fresh ginger
- 2 garlic cloves, chopped
- 1 cup diced carrots
- 1 cup diced celery
- 1 tbsp. chopped basil
- 1 tbsp. chopped coriander
- 1 tbsp. chopped mint
- 1 pinch ground black pepper
- 1 tsp turmeric
- Juice of 1 lime
- 1 cup bean sprouts
- 1 cup cooked jasmine rice
- 1 tsp. hot pepper flakes

Nutritional facts per serving

- Calories: 66cal
- Fat: 2g
- Sodium: 77mg
- Protein: 4g
- Potassium: 183mg
- Phosphorus: 49mg
- Carbohydrates: 11g

Steps

- In a pot, stir fry in 1 tbsp. of olive oil the spring onions, carrots, turmeric, garlic, ginger, and celery.
- Add the water and bring to a boil.
- Add to the boiling soup the shrimps cut into 3/3 pieces and the carrots; simmer until the shrimps are cooked and turn off the heat.
- Season the soup with the chopped herbs, hot pepper flakes and freshly ground black pepper.
- Place some cooked rice into individual cups, pour the soup and garnish with bean sprouts and lime juice.
- Serve hot.

5.12 Corn Soup

Preparation time: 15 mins

Servings: 8

Ingredients

- 8 quarts low-sodium vegetable stock
- 2 1/2 cups corn
- 2 tbsps. white vermouth
- 1 tsp. sugar
- 2 tbsps. cornstarch
- 2 egg whites
- 4 spring onions, chopped

Nutritional facts per serving

- Calories: 75cal
- Fat: 3g

- Sodium: 65mg
- Protein: 6g
- Potassium: 291mg
- Phosphorus: 62mg
- Carbohydrates: 14g

Steps

- Bring the stock to a boil, stir in the corn, and allow the stock to simmer for around five minutes.
- Strain the stock and put the liquid back into the pot. Blend the corn into a mixer.
- Strain the corn and discard any solid leftovers.
- Bring the stock to a simmer and stir in the sugar and white vermouth.
- Whisk the starch with 2 tbsp of water and add to the stock, stirring carefully until it starts to thicken.
- Lightly beat the egg whites with a whisk and add to the boiling soup, stirring for about one minute.
- Turn off the heat, pour the soup into individual bowls, garnish with the chopped spring onions and serve hot.

5.13 Beef Bourguignon

Preparation time: 1,5 hours

Servings: 4

Ingredients

- 1/2 lb. beef, cubed
- 4 onions, sliced
- 1/2 lb. portobello mushrooms, cubed
- 3 cups low sodium beef stock
- 1 carrot, diced
- 4 tbsps. fresh parsley chopped
- 1 garlic clove, shopped
- 1/2 tsp. ground black pepper
- 1 tbsp. olive oil
- 1 bacon slice
- 4 tbsps. flour
- 3 cups water
- 1 tbsp. fresh rosemary, chopped
- 1/4 cup dry red wine

Nutritional facts per serving

- Calories: 312cal
- Fat: 14g
- Sodium: 165mg
- Protein: 22g
- Potassium: 793mg
- Phosphorus: 260mg
- Carbohydrates: 23g

Steps

- In a pan, stir fry the bacon, cut into cubes, with the onions and garlic. Deglaze with the wine and put aside.
- Toss the meat cubes in the flour, discarding the excess flour. Heat the olive oil in a pot or Dutch oven and brown the meat cubes, searing them. Put the beef cubes aside.
- Add the beef stock and the water to the same pot and bring to a boil, simmering until it starts to thicken.
- Put the beef back to the pot. Add the carrot and portobello mushrooms and keep simmering uncovered for around 45 minutes.

- Add the bacon, onions and garlic cooked in advance, with all the liquid, and continue simmering for around 20 minutes. The stew should be fairly thick now.
- Pour the stew into individual dished, garnish with parsley and rosemary and serve hot.

5.14 Smoky Bean Stew

Preparation time: 40 mins

Servings: 4

Ingredients

- 1 15 oz. can of black beans, drained
- 4 spring onions, chopped
- 1/2 cup white beans, drained
- 3 cups low-sodium vegetable stock,
- 1 medium-sized carrot, chopped
- 2 tbsps. parsley, chopped
- 1 garlic clove, chopped
- 1/2 tsp. black pepper
- 1 bay leaf
- 1 tbsp. olive oil
- 1 tsp. smoked paprika
- 4 tbsps. flour
- 2 tbsps. fresh rosemary, chopped
- 1/4 cup dry red wine

Nutritional facts per serving

- Calories: 215cal
- Fat: 5g
- Sodium: 202mg
- Protein: 10g
- Potassium: 677mg
- Phosphorus: 74mg
- Carbohydrates: 43g

Steps

- Stir fry in a pot or Dutch oven the spring onions in olive oil until they start to wilt.

Add the garlic and carrot and continue stir frying for around 5 minutes.

- Add the bay leaf, pepper, smoked paprika, and all the flour.
- Deglaze the pot with the red dry wine, scraping the bottom well.
- Add the vegetable stock and bring it to a boil.
- Add the black beans, white bans and to simmer uncovered for around 30 minutes.
- Pour the stew into individual dishes, garnish with parsley and rosemary ad serve hot.

CHAPTER 6. DESSERTS

6.1 Orange & Cinnamon Biscuits

Preparation time: 50 mins

Servings: 18

Ingredients

- 2 tsps. grated orange peel
- 2 large eggs
- 2 cups all-purpose flour
- 1 tsp. vanilla extract
- 1 tsp. ground cinnamon
- 1 tsp. cream of tartar
- 1 cup sugar
- 1/2 tsp. baking soda
- 1/2 cup unsalted butter, melted

Nutritional facts per serving

- Calories: 150cal
- Fat: 7g
- Sodium: 77mg
- Protein: 3g
- Potassium: 54mg
- Phosphorus: 29mg
- Carbohydrates: 23g

Steps

- Preheat the oven to 325°F.
- Apply non-stick cooking spray to two baking sheets.
- In a large cup, mix the sugar and unsalted butter together.
- Add the eggs (one at a time), beating the mixture after each one.
- Whisk together the orange peel and the vanilla.
- In a medium-sized dish, combine the flour, cream of tartar, baking soda and cinnamon.
- Add the dry ingredients to the butter mixture and combine until blended.
- Cut the dough in two. Put each half on a sheet and shape each half into a log. Bake the dough for 35 minutes and then remove them from the oven.
- Let the bread cool for 10 minutes.
- Move the logs to the surface and cut them diagonally into half-inch-thick slices using a serrated blade.
- Proceed to bake the biscuits for 12 minutes until the bottoms become golden.
- Before serving, move them to a wire rack and allow them to cool.

6.2 Berry Bread Pudding

Preparation time: 45 mins

Servings: 10

Ingredients

- Whipped cream, for serving
- 8 cups cubed bread
- 6 eggs, beaten
- 2 tsps. vanilla
- 2 cups heavy cream

- 12 oz. frozen berries, thawed
- 1 tbsp. orange zest
- 1/2 tsp. cinnamon
- 1/2 cup sugar

Nutritional facts per serving

- Calories: 393cal
- Fat: 24g
- Sodium: 232mg
- Protein: 10g
- Potassium: 173mg
- Phosphorus: 134mg
- Carbohydrates 37g

Steps

- Preheat the oven to 375°F.
- Whisk together the eggs, sugar, cream, vanilla, orange zest, and cinnamon.
- Gently mix the cubes of bread and the fruit with your hands.
- Pour the cubes into a buttered or oiled up pan and bake them for 35 minutes.
- Take out the foil and cook the bread for an extra 15 minutes.
- Turn the oven off and let the bread sit for about 10 minutes.
- Cut and serve.

6.3 Chewy Lemon Coconut Cookies

Preparation time: 30 mins

Servings: 24

Ingredients

- 1/2 cup unsalted butter
- 1/2 cup sugar
- 1/2 tsp. baking soda
- 1 1/4 cups flour
- 1 cup toasted coconut
- 1 egg
- 1 tbsp. fresh grated ginger

- 1 tbsp. lemon zest
- 2 tbsps. lemon juice

Nutritional facts per serving

- Calories: 97cal
- Fat: 7g
- Sodium: 40mg
- Protein: 2g
- Potassium: 27mg
- Phosphorus: 17mg
- Carbohydrates: 11g

Steps

- Spread the unsweetened coconut on the baking sheet tray and bake for up to 10 minutes until the edges become light brown.
- Take it out of the oven and set it aside in a bowl.
- Mix the butter and sugar until it becomes light and fluffy with an electric mixer. Add the egg, lemon juice, lemon zest, and chopped ginger and blend until smooth.
- Sift the flour and baking soda together. Stir them in the butter mixture, whisking constantly.
- Cover the bowl and rest for a minimum of 30 minutes.
- Preheat the oven to 350°F.
- Scoop out a few tablespoons, roll them into balls, and cover them with toasted coconut flakes. Use a lightly oiled baking sheet and place the balls at a minimum of two inches apart
- Bake them for 10 to 12 minutes or until the sides become slightly brown. Remove and allow them to cool on the counter.

6.4 Cranberry Dried Fruit Bars

Preparation time: 40 mins

Servings: 24

Ingredients

Crust

- 1 1/3 cups sugar
- 3/4 cup unsalted butter (1.5 sticks)
- 1 1/2 cups all-purpose flour

Topping

- 1 cup dried cranberries
- 1 tsp. baking powder
- 1 tsp. vanilla extract
- 4 large eggs
- Powdered sugar (optional)

Nutritional facts per serving

- Calories: 191cal
- Fat: 7g
- Sodium: 34mg
- Protein: 3g
- Potassium: 28mg
- Phosphorus: 34mg
- Carbohydrates: 31g

Steps

- Preheat the oven to 350°F.
- Stir together the flour and sugar in a medium-sized bowl. Add melted unsalted butter until the mixture holds together. Pat it into a loaf and place into a 9" x 13" unoiled baking tray. Bake until it is gently browned for about 10 minutes.
- For the topping, mix the eggs, vanilla, sugar, flour, baking powder and cranberries in a medium-sized dish. Slather the topping onto the loaf. Continue baking for 20 to 25 minutes.
- While warm, cut the baked loaf into 24 bars and dust with powdered sugar.

6.5 Mint Chocolate Brownies

Preparation time: 30 mins

Servings: 12

Ingredients

- 1 box brownie mix
- 12 Andes mint chocolates

Nutritional facts per serving

- Calories: 308cal
- Fat: 18g
- Sodium: 146mg
- Protein: 4g
- Potassium: 120mg
- Phosphorus: 61mg
- Carbohydrates: 36g

Steps

- Preheat the oven at 350°F
- Prepare lightly oiled 12-cup muffin tin and add flour to both the bottom and the sides.
- Add the brownie mix to the cups and bake for about 25 minutes.
- Place a piece of mint candy in the middle of each cup and bake for an extra 5 minutes.
- Remove the brownies from the oven. Then, turn the oven off and allow the brownies to rest for 5 to 10 minutes.
- Remove them from the tin and serve.

6.6 Festive Cheese Sugar Cookies

Preparation time: 30 mins

Servings: 48

Ingredients

- 1/4 tsp. almond extract
- 1/2 tsp. vanilla extract
- 1 cup unsalted butter, softened
- 1 cup sugar
- 1 large egg, separated
- 2 1/4 cups all-purpose flour
- 3 oz. cream cheese, softened
- Colored sugar for garnishing

Nutritional facts per serving

- Calories: 80cal
- Fat: 6g
- Sodium: 34mg
- Protein: 2g
- Potassium: 12mg
- Phosphorus: 11mg
- Carbohydrates: 10g

Steps

- Mix the sugar, butter, almond extract, cream cheese, vanilla extract, and egg yolk in a large bowl. Then, add flour and whisk it in.
- Refrigerate the cookie dough for two hours.
- Proceed to preheat the oven to 350°F.
- Roll the dough on a floured surface and cut it into the desired shapes using cookie cutters.
- Place them one inch apart on unoiled cookie sheets. Keep the cookies plain or, if desired, brush them with the beaten egg white and sprinkle with colored sugar.
- Bake the cream cheese cookies for about seven to nine minutes or until they become light golden brown. Let them cool before serving.

6.7 Yellow Cake

Preparation time: 30 mins

Servings: 8

Ingredients

- 1 egg
- 1 1/2 cups of Master Mix (check recipe)
- 1/2 cup water
- 1/2 tsp. vanilla
- 2/3 cup sugar

Nutritional facts per serving

- Calories: 340cal
- Fat: 12g
- Sodium: 406mg
- Protein: 5g
- Potassium: 53mg
- Phosphorus: 225mg
- Carbohydrates: 72g

Steps

- Preheat the oven to 375°F.
- Use the Master Mix recipe and add sugar to the blend.
- In a separate dish, combine the water, egg, and vanilla.
- Pour half the liquid into the Master Mix contents and stir for two minutes.
- Then, add the remainder of the liquid and whisk everything together for two more minutes.
- Bake the cake for 25 minutes in a pan lined with parchment paper.

6.8 Sweet Berries & Mascarpone

Preparation time: 20 mins

Servings: 6

Ingredients

- 1 cup of diced strawberries
- 1 tbsp. lemon or orange zest
- 1/2 cup and 2 tsps. sugar

- 1/4 cup marsala wine or balsamic vinegar
- 2 cups mascarpone cheese

Nutritional facts per serving

- Calories: 754cal
- Fat: 9g
- Sodium: 82mg
- Protein: 12g
- Potassium: 119mg
- Phosphorus: 19mg
- Carbohydrates: 25g

Steps

- Mix the cheese, citrus zest, and 1/2 cup sugar together until they become smooth.
- Mix the berries and the balsamic vinegar with the sugar and leave it to rest for a minimum of 10 minutes.
- Divide the berries into the dessert cups and cover each with the cheese.

6.9 Angel Food Cake

Preparation time: 25 mins

Servings: 12

Ingredients

- tbsp. granulated sugar
- 1 package Angel Food cake mix
- 1/2 tsp. lemon zest
- 1/2 tsp. vanilla extract
- 1/2 pint heavy whipping cream
- 7,5 oz. chopped canned peaches (reserve the juice)
- 7,5 oz chopped canned pineapple crushed (reserve the juice)

Nutritional facts per serving

- Calories: 217cal
- Fat: 4g
- Sodium: 262mg
- Protein: 5g
- Potassium: 124mg
- Phosphorus: 132mg
- Carbohydrates: 36g

Steps

- Use the reserved juices and mix with the cake mix, in accordance with the package's directions.
- If the juice is not enough, add water.
- Fold the canned fruit into the mix and then bake according to the package's instructions.
- Use an electric mixer to combine the remaining ingredients and whisk everything until the desired consistency is achieved.
- Serve the cake with whipped cream.

6.10 Easy Cheesecake

Preparation time: 3 hours

Servings: 8

Ingredients

- 4 eggs
- 2 packs crushed crackers
- 16 oz. cream cheese, softened
- 1/2 cup sugar
- 1 tbsp. vanilla extract
- 1 stick unsalted butter, softened

Nutritional facts per serving

- Calories: 126cal
- Fat: 6g
- Sodium: 228mg
- Protein: 9g

- Potassium: 175mg
- Phosphorus: 80mg
- Carbohydrates: 13g

Steps

- Preheat the oven to 325°F.
- Mix the butter and the crushed crackers until they are completely combined. Spread the mixture evenly on the bottom of a pan.
- Whisk the cream cheese, eggs, sugar, and vanilla until they are completely mixed. Pour the mixture onto the crust. Proceed to bake the cake for about 45 to 60 minutes or until the center no longer jiggles.
- Let the mixture cool for three hours.
- Try topping with your favorite sauce.

6.11 Strawberries Brulèe

Preparation time: 10 mins

Servings: 8

Ingredients

- 6 oz. of cream cheese
- 1/4 cup and 2 tbsps. brown sugar, divided and packed
- 1 quart fresh strawberries
- 1 cup sour cream

Nutritional facts per serving

- Calories: 188cal
- Fat: 8g
- Sodium: 69mg
- Protein: 4g
- Potassium: 208mg
- Phosphorus: 60mg
- Carbohydrates: 10g

Steps

- Blend the cream cheese with an electric mixer until it softens. Then, add two tablespoons of brown sugar and the sour cream. Beat until they become smooth.

- Cut the strawberries in half and arrange them uniformly in a shallow, circular, eight-inch-long broiler proof dish.
- Cover the berries with the cream mixture.
- Sprinkle the leftover quarter cup of brown sugar over the cream mixture.
- Broil for one to two minutes or until the sugar becomes golden brown.
- Serve immediately.

6.12 Squash Cookies

Preparation time: 20 mins

Servings: 30

Ingredients

- 1 1/2 cups cooked winter squash, mashed
- 1 1/2 cups pecans or walnuts, chopped
- 1 cup raisins
- 1 tsp. baking soda
- 1 tsp. cinnamon
- 1/2 cup softened butter
- 1/2 tsp. ground cardamom
- 1/4 tsp. allspice
- 1/4 tsp. ground ginger
- 2 1/2 cups flour
- 2 1/2 tsps. baking powder
- 2 eggs
- 1 1/2 cups brown sugar

Nutritional facts per serving

- Calories: 85cal
- Fat: 4g
- Sodium: 126mg
- Protein: 3g
- Potassium: 161mg
- Phosphorus: 55mg
- Carbohydrates: 8g

Steps

- Preheat the oven to 375°F.
- Mix the butter and sugar until they become fluffy.
- Beat the eggs together.

- Then, mix together the dry ingredients and stir in the eggs, butter and sugar; add the mashed squash to the mixture.
- Whisk in the nuts and raisins.
- Spoon the mixture onto a baking sheet and bake for 10 to 12 minutes.

6.13 Vanilla Cream Sauce

Preparation time: 30 mins

Servings: 6

Ingredients

- 1 1/2 cups milk
- 1 vanilla bean, halved lengthwise
- 2 tbsps. cornstarch
- 3 egg yolks
- 3 tbsps. of granulated sugar
- 2 tbsps. brandy (optional)

Nutritional facts per serving

- Calories: 68.8cal
- Fat: 0.6g
- Sodium: 51.8mg
- Protein: 2.1g
- Potassium: 112mg
- Phosphorus: 87mg
- Carbohydrates: 33.8g

Steps

- Use two beans if you are recycling vanilla beans from a different recipe.
- Use a sharp knife to scrape the pods off the vanilla bean and put them in a small saucepan with the milk.
- Allow the milk to simmer at medium-high heat but do not let it boil. Continue to stir occasionally.
- Remove the milk from the heat and let it cool.
- Whisk in the milk the egg yolks, and cornstarch.
- Boil the milk over high heat, constantly whisking.
- Check the mixture with the back of a spoon and see if it becomes coated with a thin layer. If yes, this indicates that it's thickening. Once it thickens, it should be ready.
- Pour the sauce quickly in a ceramic or metal bowl and let it cool and reach room temperature, stirring occasionally.
- You can add the liquor to it when the cream cools (if desired).

6.14 Rhubarb Pie

Preparation time: 1 hour

Servings: 8

Ingredients

- 4 cups unpeeled rhubarb stalks, diced
- 2 eggs
- 1/4 cup flour
- 1 tsp. grated orange rind
- 1 tbsp. butter
- 1 recipe pie crust (double crust)
- 2 cups sugar

Nutritional facts per serving

- Calories: 386cal
- Fat: 10g
- Sodium: 121mg
- Protein: 3g
- Potassium: 90mg
- Phosphorous: 21mg
- Carbohydrates: 21g

Steps

- Preheat the oven to 450°F.
- Whisk eggs with butter, flour and sugar until
- it becomes very creamy and gently add the diced rhubarb.
- Let the mixture rest for 15 minutes, then pour in a pie shell.
- Sprinkle with orange rind and put the pie into the preheated oven.
- Bake for about 10 minutes, and then reduce the heat to 350°F, letting the pie bake for another 45 minutes.
- Take the pie out of the oven, let cool and serve.

6.15 Raspberry Bavarian Pie

Preparation time: 30 mins

Servings: 12

Ingredients

- 2 egg whites
- 2 1/2 tbsps. sugar
- 10 oz. fresh raspberries, mashed
- 1/4 tsp. vanilla
- 1/4 tsp. almond extract
- 1/3 cup butter
- 1/3 cup chopped almonds
- 1 tbsp. lemon juice
- 1 egg yolk
- 1 cup sugar
- 1 cup whipping cream
- 1 cup flour

Nutritional facts per serving

- Calories: 268cal
- Fat: 4g
- Sodium: 60mg
- Protein: 4g
- Potassium: 77mg
- Phosphorus: 39mg
- Carbohydrates: 33g

Steps

- Preheat the oven to 400°F.
- Oil a 10-inch pie pan.
- Whisk the butter with 2 1/2 tablespoons of sugar until the mixture becomes fluffy.
- Add the egg yolk and thoroughly mix everything together, before adding the flour and almonds.
- In a prepared pie pan, press and bake the crust for 12 minutes.
- Place the rest of the ingredients in a large bowl for the filling, with the exception of the whipping cream.
- Beat the mixture until it thickens and increases in volume.
- Whip and fold the cream into the raspberry mixture.
- Then, add it to the pastry and refrigerate it for 8 or more hours.

6.16 Pumpkin Mousse Pie

Preparation time: 4 hours

Servings: 8

Ingredients

- 3/4 cup milk
- 3 1/2 cups non-dairy cool whipped topping
- 1/2 cup canned pumpkin
- 1/2 tsp. ginger
- 1/2 tsp. cinnamon
- 1/2 tsp. ground cardamom
- 1 small package vanilla pudding
- 1 baked, cooled pie shell

Nutritional facts per serving

- Calories: 239cal
- Fat: 9g
- Sodium: 295mg
- Protein: 3g
- Potassium: 111mg
- Phosphorus: 129mg
- Carbohydrates: 31g

Steps

- Add the milk to the pudding mix and beat it for about two minutes or until it thickens.
- Mix in the pumpkin and the spices.
- Proceed to fold the cool whip into two cups of the whipped topping and spread the mixture into the pie shell.
- Refrigerate it for at least four hours. Serve with the remaining cool whip.

6.17 Popcorn Balls

Preparation time: 20 mins

Servings: 18

Ingredients

- 1 tsp. butter
- 1 tsp. vinegar
- 2 cups sugar
- 1 tsp. vanilla
- 1 1/2 cups water
- 1/2 cup light corn syrup
- 4 quarts of popped popcorn
- 1 tsp. butter for making the balls

Nutritional facts per serving

- Calories: 147cal
- Fat: 2g
- Sodium: 8mg
- Protein: 2g
- Potassium: 28mg
- Phosphorus: 30mg
- Carbohydrates: 37g

Steps

- Add butter to the sides of a medium-sized saucepan.
- Add water, syrup, sugar, and vinegar to the pan.
- Leave it to boil, stirring over medium-high heat, stirring occasionally.

- Remove from the heat and whisk in the vanilla.
- Place the popcorn in a large bowl and pour the syrup over it.
- Let the mixture cool until your hands are ready to handle it.
- Grease your hands and form the popcorn balls.

6.18 Pear Cardamom Cake

Preparation time: 40 mins

Servings: 8

Ingredients

- 1 1/2 cups all-purpose flour
- 1 1/2 tsps. low-sodium baking powder
- 1 egg
- 1 tsp. vanilla
- 1/2 cup sugar
- 1/4 cup unsalted butter
- 2 tsps. ground cardamom
- 2/3 cup unsalted butter
- 3/4 cup cream
- 3/4 cup sugar
- 4 pears

Nutritional facts per serving

- Calories: 443cal
- Fat: 4g
- Sodium: 25mg
- Protein: 6g
- Potassium: 251mg
- Phosphorus: 138mg
- Carbohydrates: 59g

Steps

- Heat the oven to 350°F.
- Peel the pears, remove the core, and cut them into quarters. In a big, non-stick pan, melt a quarter cup of butter. Stir in the 1/2 cup of sugar.

- Add the pears to the mixture.
- Cover and cook for around 15 minutes on medium-high heat, checking it periodically to prevent burning
- Meanwhile, beat two-thirds of a cup of butter and three-fourths of a cup of sugar with the electric mixer or a food processor until the mixture becomes light and fluffy.
- Stir in the vanilla and egg and cream. Mix the flour with the cardamom and baking powder. Then, fold the dry ingredients into the egg mixture with the spatula.
- Place the pears and their sauce into a 8x9"-long glass cake pan, leaving the fruit face down. Pour the batter uniformly over the pears.
- Bake in the oven for about 20 to 25 minutes until it becomes golden brown.
- Allow the cake to cool for five minutes before cutting.
- Serve immediately or when desired.

6.19 Pavlova Meringue Cake

Preparation time: 3 hours

Servings: 8

Ingredients

- 1 cup whipping cream
- 1 tbsp. cornstarch
- 1 tsp. vanilla extract
- 1 tsp. white vinegar
- 1/4 tsps. vanilla extract
- 2 cups fresh strawberries
- 2 tbsps. granulated sugar
- 3/4 cup granulated sugar
- 4 egg whites

Nutritional facts per serving

- Calories: 212cal
- Fat: 11g
- Sodium: 40mg
- Protein: 4g
- Potassium: 118mg
- Phosphorus: 30mg
- Carbohydrates: 27g

Steps

- Preheat the oven to 350°F.
- Use parchment paper to cover a cake tin.
- Beat the egg whites with an electric mixer until rigid peaks form.
- Add sugar slowly and beat for four to five minutes or until the mixture becomes stiff.
- Add 1 tsp. of vanilla extract, vinegar, and cornstarch to the egg whites and whip them until they are well mixed together.
- Spread the white egg mixture in the tin to create an 8"-wide circle, like a shallow cup, leaving the outer edges slightly elevated.
- Place the cake batter in the oven and reduce the heat to 200°F. Leave it in the oven for one hour.
- Turn the oven off and leave the cake in it to cool for one hour with the door open.
- Whisk together two tablespoons of sugar,
- whipping cream, and 1/4 tsp. vanilla until stiff peaks are formed.
- Cover the cool meringue with the whipped cream and top with the fruit.

6.20 Lemon Curd

Preparation time: 20 mins

Servings: 2

Ingredients

- Zest of 4 lemons
- 4 whole eggs, well beaten
- 2/3 cup lemon juice
- 2 cups granulated sugar
- 1 cup unsalted butter

Nutritional facts per serving

- Calories: 100cal
- Fat: 3g
- Sodium: 10mg
- Protein: 2g
- Potassium: 16mg
- Phosphorus: 14mg
- Carbohydrates: 13g

Steps

- Heat the lemon juice, sugar, and zests in a saucepan until the sugar has dissolved.
- Remove the mixture from the pan and add butter. Wait for it to melt.
- When the mixture reaches room temperature, gently fold in the eggs.
- Return the mixture to the heat over a double boiler. When the mixture thickens, remove it from the heat and pour through a fine strainer.
- Refrigerate and serve.

6.21 Lemon Chess Pie

Preparation time: 1 hour

Servings: 8

Ingredients

- 6 tbsps. unsalted butter
- 4 large eggs
- 3 tbsps. cornstarch
- 2 tbsps. lemon zest
- 1/3 cup fresh lemon juice
- 1 cup whipped cream
- 1 sheet pie crust
- 1 1/2 cups sugar
- Fresh mint sprigs

Nutritional facts per serving

- Preheat the oven to 350°F.
- Bake a pie crust for around eight minutes or according to the box's instruction, until it becomes golden brown. Allow it to cool.
- In a large cup, beat the sugar and butter until it is light and fluffy. Then, add the lemon zest, lemon juice and cornstarch.
- Add the eggs (one at a time) and continue whisking with every addition.
- Spoon the mixture into the shell of the crust.
- Bake until the filling becomes set and the top turns golden brown (40 to 45 minutes).
- Cool and serve with whipped cream and a little sprig of mint.

6.22 Almond Plum Pie

Preparation time: 50 mins

Servings: 8

Ingredients

- 1/4 tsps. almond extract
- 1/2 cup sugar
- Lemon zest
- 1/2 package (4 oz.) almond paste or marzipan
- 1/2 tsp. cinnamon
- 1 pre-made pie crust
- 4 cups plums
- 6 tbsps. Cornstarch

Nutritional facts per serving

- Calories: 271cal

- Fat: 11g
- Sodium: 93mg
- Protein: 4g
- Potassium: 201mg
- Phosphorus: 67mg
- Carbohydrates: 45g

Steps

- Cut the plums in half and remove the pits.
- Combine the almond extract, sugar, lemon zest, cinnamon, cornstarch and plums in a bowl. Add the diced marzipan and mix well.
- Place the pie crust in a 9"-long dish. Pour in the filling and bake for 35 to 45 minutes at 425°F.

6.23 Easy Ice Cream

Preparation time: 15 mins

Servings: 4

Ingredients

- 1 1/2 cups frozen fruit of your choice
- 1/2 cup sugar
- 1 cup whipping cream

Nutritional facts per serving

- Calories: 279cal
- Fat: 16g
- Sodium: 24mg
- Protein: 3g

- Potassium: 82mg
- Phosphorus: 38mg
- Carbohydrates: 22g

Steps

- Make sure the fruit is frozen (do not thaw it).
- Add all the ingredients to the food processor and pulse until the mixture becomes fluffy and very thick.
- Serve immediately.

6.24 Ginger Cookies

Preparation time: 20 mins

Servings: 36

Ingredients

- 3/4 cup unsalted butter
- 2 tsps. baking soda
- 2 tsps. fresh ginger (finely grated)
- 2 cups flour
- 1/4 cup dark molasses
- 1/3 cup cinnamon sugar
- 1/2 cup candied ginger (finely chopped)
- 1 tsp. cinnamon
- 1 tbsp. ground ginger
- 1 egg
- 1 cup granulated sugar

Nutritional facts per serving

- Calories: 93cal
- Fat: 4g
- Sodium: 118mg
- Protein: 2g
- Potassium: 58mg
- Phosphorus: 12mg
- Carbohydrates: 15g

Steps

- Preheat the oven to 350°F.

- In a mixing cup, combine the flour, baking soda, ginger, and cinnamon.
- Add the butter and beat until smooth. Pour in 1 cup of granulated sugar slowly, then add the molasses and egg.
- Mix thoroughly, then, add the candied ginger.
- Pinch off a small amount of the mix and roll into small balls.
- Wrap each ball in cinnamon sugar and put it on an unoiled baking sheet, two inches apart from each other.
- Bake in a preheated oven for about 10 minutes until the tops become rounded and lightly cracked.
- Allow the cookies to cool on a wire rack.
- Serve immediately or store in an air-tight jar for later.

6.25 Dessert Pizza

Preparation time: 20 mins

Servings: 8

Ingredients

- 1 12"-long precooked pizza crust
- 1 cup of low-fat ricotta cheese
- 1/4 cup chocolate chips
- 1/2 cup apricot jam
- 2 cups fresh sliced strawberry
- 5 tbsps. divided powdered sugar

Nutritional facts per serving

- Calories: 289cal
- Fat: 11g
- Sodium: 167mg
- Protein: 9g
- Potassium: 99mg
- Phosphorus: 48mg
- Carbohydrates: 50g

Steps

- Preheat the oven to 425°F.
- Strain the ricotta with a cheesecloth
- Heat the jam for 30 seconds in the microwave.
- Mix the ricotta with the jam, strawberries, and three teaspoons of powdered sugar.
- Pour the mix onto the pizza crust.
- Sprinkle with the chocolate chips and leftover powdered sugar.
- Bake for about 10 to 12 minutes.

6.26 Carrot Muffins

Preparation time: 30 mins

Servings: 12

Ingredients

- 2 large eggs
- 2 cups shredded carrots (about 6 medium-sized carrots)
- 1/2 cup all-purpose flour
- 1/2 cup whole wheat flour
- 1/2 cup oats
- 1/2 cup brown sugar
- 1/2 cup vegetable oil
- 1/2 cup unsweetened applesauce
- 3/4 tsps. baking powder
- 3/4 tsps. baking soda
- 3/4 tsps. Cinnamon

Nutritional facts per serving

- Calories: 207cal
- Fat: 13g
- Sodium: 136mg
- Protein: 5g
- Potassium: 143mg
- Phosphorus: 99mg
- Carbohydrates: 24g

Steps

- Preheat the oven to 350°F.
- Coat the muffin tins lightly with non-stick spray.
- In a big dish, mix the dry ingredients together.
- Mix the wet ingredients in a medium-sized bowl with a whisk and then combine with the dry ingredients.
- Combine with the shredded carrots and cover the muffins with the batter.
- Bake the muffins for about 20 minutes.

CHAPTER 7. VEGETARIAN DISHES

7.1 Vegan Breakfast Rice

Preparation time: 30 mins

Servings: 4

Ingredients

- 1 cup jasmine rice
- 2 tbsps. olive oil
- 1 cup cooked chickpeas
- 1 1/2 cups broccoli florets
- 2 tbsps. smoked paprika
- 1/2 tsp. cumin
- 1/4 tsp. powdered garlic
- 1/4 tsps. powdered onion
- 2 tbsps. chopped coriander
- 1/4 tsp. black pepper
- 1/4 cup of low-sodium vegetable stock
- 1/2 lime cut into 4 wedges

Nutritional facts per serving

- Calories: 347cal
- Fat: 13g
- Sodium: 291mg
- Protein: 9g
- Potassium: 455mg
- Phosphorus: 133mg
- Carbohydrates: 53g

Steps

- Cook the rice in accordance with the box's instructions.
- In a wide pan, heat the oil and stir fry the broccoli. Add the chickpeas, paprika, cumin, garlic powder, onion powder and pepper. Add the stock and cook until the broccoli is tender.
- Pour the rice into four individual platters. Cover the rice with the chickpeas and broccoli preparation, garnish with chopped coriander and a lime wedge and serve.

7.2 Savory Crustless Pie

Preparation time: 1 hour

Servings: 4

Ingredients

- 1 cup milk
- 3 eggs
- 1/2 cup all-purpose flour
- 3 pieces bacon, chopped
- 1 cup spring onions, chopped
- 1 cup portobello mushrooms,
- chopped
- 1 cup green beans, chopped

Nutritional facts per serving

- Calories: 196cal
- Fat: 8g
- Sodium: 176mg
- Protein: 13g
- Potassium: 345mg
- Phosphorus: 195mg
- Carbohydrates: 23g

Steps

- Pre-heat the oven at 350°F.
- Whisk the eggs, flower and milk in a bowl, mixing thoroughly until smooth.
- Stir fry in a pan the bacon, onions, mushrooms for about 10 minutes; add the

green beans and continue cooking until desired.

- Apply cooking spray to an 8×8" baking pan. Spread the cooked vegetables and bacon on the bottom of the pan and cover with the egg mix. Cook for about 30/35 minutes until the pie is set and golden brown.

7.3 Peach and Strawberry Smoothie

Preparation time: 5 minutes

Servings: 3

Ingredients

- 1 cup frozen strawberries
- 1 peach, pitted and cubed
- 1/2 cup diced soft tofu
- 1 tbsp. agave syrup
- 1 cup rice milk

Nutritional facts per serving

- Calories: 130cal
- Fat: 4g
- Sodium: 54mg
- Protein: 7g
- Potassium: 262mg
- Phosphorus: 73mg
- Carbohydrates: 24g

Steps

- In a mixer, combine all the ingredients until creamy and serve.

7.4 Maple Seitan Sausage

Preparation time: 20 minutes

Servings: 12

Ingredients

- 1 1/2 lb. ground seitan
- 1/2 tsp. black pepper
- 3/4 tsp. dry rosemary
- 1 pinch of nutmeg
- 1 tsp. smoked paprika
- 4 tbsps. parsley, chopped
- 2 tsps. maple syrup

- 1 tsp. water

Nutritional facts per serving

- Calories: 153cal
- Fat: 9g
- Sodium: 44mg
- Protein: 14g
- Potassium: 184mg
- Phosphorus: 130mg
- Carbohydrates: 2g

Steps

- In a large container, combine all the ingredients together.
- Refrigerate the seitan mix overnight or for at least four hours.
- Preheat the oven at 400°F
- Shape the mix into patties and bake in a skillet until it browns, around 15 minutes.

7.5 Spiced Paratha

Preparation time: 25 minutes

Servings: 2

Ingredients

- 2 cups wheat flour
- 1 cup of water for kneading
- 1/2 tsp. cumin seeds
- 1/4 tsp. ground dry coriander
- 1/4 tsp. ground turmeric
- 1 tsp. oil

Nutritional facts per serving

- Calories: 133cal
- Fat: 3g
- Sodium: 1mg
- Protein: 1g
- Potassium: 129mg
- Phosphorus: 100mg
- Carbohydrates: 22g

Steps

- Knead in a bowl the flower, spices and water, until smooth; cover with cling film and let rest for around half an hour.
- Knead the dough and leave it to rest for 20 minutes.
- Divide the dough into 4 parts and shape like balls.
- Flatten the balls into paratha using a rolling pin and cook over a hot iron plate or pan.

7.6 Pineapple and Pepper Curry

Preparation time: 20 minutes

Servings: 4

Ingredients

- 4 red peppers, chopped
- 1 medium-sized red onion, chopped
- 1 tbsp. fresh mint, chopped
- 8 cherry tomatoes, quartered
- 1 tbsp. minced ginger
- 2 tsps. olive oil
- 1/2 cup canned pineapple, drained
- and chopped
- 1 tsp. curry powder
- 1 tsp. ground turmeric
- 1 lime cut into wedges

Nutritional facts per serving

- Calories: 110cal
- Fat: 8g
- Sodium: 10mg
- Protein: 2g
- Potassium: 234mg
- Phosphorus: 27mg
- Carbohydrates: 11g

Steps

- Heat the oil in a pan and stir fry the ginger, curry powder, turmeric, red onion and peppers for around 15 minutes, until slightly browned.
- Add the pineapple and tomatoes, cooking for 5 more minutes, until the flavors are well combined.
- Turn off the heat, sprinkle with chopped mint and serve garnishing with lime wedges.

7.7 Spicy Veggie Curry with Naan Bread

Preparation time: 30 minutes

Servings: 6

Ingredients

- 2 tbsps. olive oil
- 2 spring onions, diced
- 1/2 cup zucchini, diced
- 1/2 cup broccoli florets
- 1/2 cup green peppers, diced
- 1 cup cooked quinoa
- 2 tbsps. fresh lemon juice
- 2 tbsps. fresh cilantro, chopped
- 1/2 cup queso fresco or paneer
- 6 small naan breads
- 2 tbsps. curry powder
- 1 lime cut into 6 wedges

Nutritional facts per serving

- Calories: 307cal

- Fat: 15g
- Sodium: 405mg
- Protein: 13g
- Potassium: 282mg
- Phosphorus: 239mg
- Carbohydrates: 37g

Steps

- Heat the olive oil to medium-high heat in a wide pan and stir fry the curry powder, spring onions, zucchini, broccoli, and green peppers. Sauté for about 15 minutes until lightly browned.
- Add the cooked quinoa, cheese, mix and turn off the heat.
- Garnish with the chopped cilantro, lime wedges and serve with warm naan bread.

7.8 Red Cabbage Casserole

Preparation time: 30 minutes

Servings: 6

Ingredients

- 4 cups red cabbage, chopped
- 1 cup spring onions, chopped
- 3 red apples, cored and cubed
- 1/4 cup lemon juice
- 1/4 cup water
- 2 tbsps. sugar
- 1 tsps. ground turmeric
- 1 pinch black pepper
- 4 tbsps. parsley, chopped
- 2 tbsps. olive oil

Nutritional facts per serving

- Calories: 81cal
- Fat: 4g
- Sodium: 14mg
- Protein: 2g
- Potassium: 162mg
- Phosphorus: 24mg
- Carbohydrates: 14g

Steps

- Preheat the oven to 300°F.
- In a large bowl, combine all the ingredients and mix thoroughly.

- Place the seasoned vegetables it in a wide baking tray and let bake for one and a half hours.
- Take the tray out of the oven, add the chopped parsley, mix, and serve.

7.9 Parsley, Lime, and Mustard Marinade

Preparation time: 40 minutes

Servings: 6

Ingredients

- 1/2 cup lime juice
- 3 tbsps. french mustard
- 2 tbsps. honey
- 1 tbsp. fresh parsley, chopped

Nutritional facts per serving

- Calories: 36cal
- Fat: 1g
- Sodium: 181mg
- Protein: 1g
- Potassium: 47mg
- Phosphorus: 3mg
- Carbohydrates: 10g

Steps

- Mix together the lime juice, mustard, honey, and chopped in a big bowl.
- Whisk the marinade thoroughly, until the mustard and honey are dissolved.
- Use the mix to marinade mixed vegetables for at least 30 minutes before direct grilling on coals or baking in the oven.

7.10 Cabbage-Pepper Medley

Preparation time: 15 minutes

Servings: 4

Ingredients

- 1 1/2 cup mixed bell peppers,
- chopped
- 1/2 cup spring onions, chopped
- 2 cups white cabbage, shredded
- 3 tbsps. lemon juice

- 1 tbsp. olive oil
- 1 1/2 tsps. honey
- 1 1/2 tsps. french mustard
- 1 pinch black pepper
- 4 tbsps. parsley, chopped

Nutritional facts per serving

- Calories: 71cal
- Fat: 5g
- Sodium: 53mg
- Protein: 2g
- Potassium: 210mg
- Phosphorus: 30mg
- Carbohydrates: 9g

Steps

- In a wide pan, stir fry for around 15 minutes the peppers, spring onions and cabbage in 1 tbsp. olive oil.
- Add the lemon juice, honey and mustard and sauté until the flavors are combined.
- Season with a pinch of pepper, add the chopped parsley, mix and serve hot.

7.11 Mexican Tofu Dumplings

Preparation time: 50 minutes

Servings: 12

Ingredients

- 2 lbs. firm tofu, cubed
- 48 small wonton wrappers

Marinade

- 3 tbsps. smoked paprika
- 1 tbsp. oregano
- 3 tbsps. fresh cilantro, chopped
- 1 tsp. black pepper
- 1 tsp. red pepper flakes
- 1/2 cup lime juice
- 1/4 cup olive oil

Side mix

- 1/2 cup vegetable mayonnaise
- 2 garlic cloves, chopped
- 4 tbsps. spring onions, chopped
- 4 tbsps. coriander, chopped

- 4 cups of shredded cabbage
- 1/4 cup lime juice

Nutritional facts per serving

- Calories: 255cal
- Fat: 10g
- Sodium: 273mg
- Protein: 12g
- Potassium: 270mg
- Phosphorus: 117mg
- Carbohydrates: 23g

Steps

- Preheat the oven to 400°F.
- Whisk the marinade components and set it aside.
- Marinate the tofu cubes for half an hour in half a cup of the marinade.
- Bake the tofu at 400°F for 15 minutes in the oven. Remove the tofu, set aside and lower the oven temperature at 350°F
- Whisk in a bowl the mayonnaise, the remaining marinade, garlic, green onions and coriander. Add the shredded cabbage and mix thoroughly to get all the flavors combined.
- Apply cooking spray to a miniature muffin tray and use one wonton wrapper to cover the muffin cups.
- Bake at 350°F for five minutes. Allow it to cool and remove the dumplings
- Distribute the tofu and side mix on the dumplings, sprinkle with coriander leaves and serve.

7.12 Sweet and Crunchy Salad

Preparation time: 10 minutes

Servings: 12

Ingredients

- 6 cups cabbage, chopped
- 1/2 cup spring onions, finely chopped
- 1 cup sugar
- 1 cup olive oil
- 1 tsp. nigella seeds
- 1/2 cup lime juice
- 1 tsp. french mustard

Nutritional facts per serving

- Calories: 245cal
- Fat: 20g
- Sodium: 13mg
- Protein: 2g
- Potassium: 74mg
- Phosphorus: 14mg
- Carbohydrates: 21g

Steps

- Place the cabbage and onion in a wide bowl.
- Whisk all the other ingredients until combined.
- Add the dressing to the bowl, mix thoroughly and refrigerate for at least half an hour.
- Serve cold.

7.13 Pumpkin Strudel

Preparation time: 30 minutes

Servings: 8

Ingredients

- 1 pinch powdered cardamom
- 4 tbsp olive oil
- 1/2 tsp. powdered cinnamon
- 1 tsp. vanilla extract
- 1 1/2 cups canned sodium-free pumpkin
- 2 sheets phyllo dough, defrosted
- 4 tbsps. brown sugar

Nutritional facts per serving

- Calories: 181cal
- Fat: 9g
- Sodium: 142mg
- Protein: 4g
- Potassium: 120mg
- Phosphorus: 40mg
- Carbohydrates: 27g

Steps

- Preheat the oven to 375°F.
- Combine the cardamom, half the cinnamon, vanilla extract, pumpkin, two tablespoons of brown sugar, in a medium-sized bowl.

- With a brush, cover the bottom of the non-stick medium-sheet tray with olive oil. Stack every phyllo sheet above one another, brushing a little oil over each sheet.
- Distribute the mix from the bowl above the phyllo pastry, trying to shape a loaf and roll the pastry to close the strudel.
- Add to the top any leftover oil.
- Blend the remaining sugar and cinnamon and sprinkle it over the strudel.
- Bake until golden brown, around 15 minutes, take out of the oven and let cool.
- Cut the strudel and serve warm or cold.

7.14 Cinnamon-Apple Phyllo Pastries

Preparation time: 25 minutes

Servings: 6

Ingredients

- 4 apples, cored peeled and chopped
- 2 tbsps. vanilla extract
- 2 tbsps. oil
- 1 tsp. cinnamon
- 6 phyllo sheets
- 1/4 tsp. cardamom
- 1/4 tsp. cornstarch
- 4 tbsps. light brown sugar
- 1/4 cup olive oil, to brush the phyllo dough
- 2 tbsps. cinnamon
- 3 tbsps. icing sugar
- Fresh mint leaves

Nutritional facts per serving

- Calories: 281cal
- Fat: 14g
- Sodium: 98mg
- Protein: 3g
- Potassium: 178mg
- Phosphorus: 34mg
- Carbohydrates: 39g

Steps

- Preheat the oven to 350°F.
- Sauté the apples in the oil for six to eight minutes in a wide saucepan over medium high heat.
- Stir in the cinnamon, brown sugar, and cardamom. Cook until the sugar start caramelizing.
- Mix the cornstarch and vanilla extract in a small cup until it is dissolved. Add to apple and cook for 3 more minutes.
- Turn off the heat and set the mixture aside.
- Lightly oil a large six-muffin tin pan.
- Stack every phyllo sheet above one another, brushing a little oil over each sheet and sprinkling with a little icing sugar and cinnamon.
- Cut the stack into six squares. Line the bottom and sides of every muffin cup, with a square of phyllo stacked dough.
- Fill up each cup with the apple mixture until it is three-quarters full.
- Fold any extra phyllo dough over the apples.
- Bake the cups for up to 10 minutes at 350°F in the preheated oven or until they become golden brown.

7.15 Lime Bars

Preparation time: 40 minutes

Servings: 24

Ingredients

Crust

- 2 cups all-purpose flour
- 1 cup soft butter
- 1/2 cup icing sugar

Filling

- 4 eggs
- 1 1/2 cups sugar
- 1/2 tsp. cream of tartar
- 1 1/2 tsp. baking soda
- 4 tbsps. lime juice
- 4 tbsps. all-purpose flour

Glaze

- 1 cup icing sugar
- 2 tbsps. lime juice

Nutritional facts per serving

- Calories: 202cal
- Fat: 10g
- Sodium: 28mg
- Protein: 3g
- Potassium: 42mg
- Phosphorus: 32mg
- Carbohydrates: 28g

Steps

Crust

- Preheat the oven to 350°F.
- Combine the icing sugar, flour, and softened butter in a large bowl. Mix until it becomes crumbly. In a 9x13" baking pan, press the mixture down to form a crust.
- Bake the bars for about 15 to 20 minutes, until lightly browned.

Filling

- Whisk the eggs in a bowl.
- Combine the sugar, flour, cream of tartar, and baking soda in another dish. Add the eggs and lime juice and whisk thoroughly until combined.
- Pour the mixture over the crust and bake until set, around 20/25 minutes.
- Take the baking pan out of the oven and allow it to cool.

Glaze

- Whisk the lime juice into the powdered sugar in a small bowl until it thickens.
- Spread the glaze over the cake, let it set and cut into 24 pieces.

7.16 Cardamom Rice Pudding

Preparation time: 20 minutes

Servings: 4

Ingredients

- 3 oz. sugar
- 3 1/2 oz. rice
- 1 tsp. vanilla essence
- 1 tsp. cardamom
- 1 1/2 cup rice milk
- 1 cup water
- 1 cup vegetable heavy cream

Nutritional facts per serving

- Calories: 587cal
- Fat: 23g
- Sodium: 100mg
- Protein: 6g
- Potassium: 192mg
- Phosphorus: 137mg
- Carbohydrates: 47g

Steps

- Place the sugar, rice, milk, water and half and half in a saucepan and bring to a gentle simmer. Cook over low heat for an hour, constantly stirring.
- When the rice is very soft, whisk in vanilla essence and cardamom to taste.
- Scoop the pudding into individual cups and serve warm.

7.17 Slow Cooker Pineapple Cherry Cake

Preparation time: 3 hours

Servings: 10

Ingredients

- 1 tbsp. melted butter
- 1 tsp. cinnamon
- 1 lb. yellow cake mix
- 1/2 cup soft butter
- 1 lb. chunk of tinned pineapple
- 1 lb. tinned red cherries

Nutritional facts per serving

- Calories: 450cal
- Fat: 12g
- Sodium: 330mg
- Protein: 5g
- Potassium: 231mg
- Phosphorus: 222mg
- Carbohydrates: 71g

Steps

- Set up a dutch oven or slow cooker and brush 1 tbsp. of melted butter on the bottom and sides.
- Place a layer of pineapple chunks, then a layer of cherries and, at last, a layer of cake mix, sprinkling a little cinnamon over each layer.
- Scatter soft butter dollops over the cake surface.
- Cover the cooker and cook for 2/3 hour on high heat.

7.18 Rhubarb Cakes

Preparation time: 1 hour

Servings: 12

Ingredients

- 1 cup all-purpose flour
- 1 tsp. cinnamon
- 1 cup brown sugar
- 4 cups tinned rhubarb
- 1 cup granulated sugar
- 1 cup water
- 3 tbsps. cornstarch
- 1/2 cup melted, unsalted butter
- 1 cup oatmeal

Nutritional facts per serving

- Calories: 252cal
- Fat: 8g
- Sodium: 9mg
- Protein: 3g
- Potassium: 193mg
- Phosphorus: 47mg
- Carbohydrates: 45g

Steps

- Preheat the oven to 350°F.
- Mix the flour, oatmeal, brown sugar, and cinnamon in a bowl.
- Add the melted butter to the bowl and blend until it gets crumbly.
- Add 2/3 of the mix to a 9×9"-long square pan, pressing to make the cake crust, and spread over it the chopped rhubarb.
- In a skillet, boil the water with the granulated sugar and cornstarch, until the mixture thickens.
- Pour the hot mixture over the cake and sprinkle the leftover flour and oatmeal mix over the surface.
- Bake for around 50/60 minutes, until the surface is golden brown.
- Take the cake out of the oven, let rest for a little and serve warm or cold.

7.19 Chocolate Fudge

Preparation time: 15 mins

Servings: 48

Ingredients

- 1 tsp. baking soda
- 2 cans sweet, condensed milk
- 2 cups cashews, chopped
- 2 tbsps. vanilla extract
- 4 cups chocolate chips
- 1 oz. bitter chocolate, crumbled

Nutritional facts per serving

- Calories: 191cal
- Fat: 2g
- Sodium: 63mg
- Protein: 4g
- Potassium: 173mg
- Phosphorus: 95mg
- Carbohydrates: 23g

Steps

- Spray with non-stick spray the bottom of a 10×14"-inch tray.
- Pour all the ingredients, except the cashews, into a glass bowl.

- Microwave on high until the chocolate starts to melt.
- Take the bowl out of the oven and mix thoroughly with a rubber spatula until completely melted.
- Add the chopped cashews, stir well and spread on the tray. Refrigerate for about 3 hours or overnight.
- Cut it into squares and serve.

7.20 Cream Cheese Spread

Preparation time: 10 mins

Servings: 5

Ingredients

- 20 slices toasted bread
- 2 tbsps. water
- 2 tbsps. spring onions, minced
- 1 cup soft cream cheese
- 1 garlic clove
- 1/2 tsp. freshly ground black pepper
- 1/4 cup mixed chopped fresh parsley, dill and thyme

Nutritional facts per serving

- Calories: 80cal
- Fat: 3g
- Sodium: 173mg
- Protein: 3g
- Potassium: 63mg
- Phosphorus: 48mg
- Carbohydrates: 11g

Steps

- In a blender, mix the cheese, water, herbs, spring onions, pepper.
- Rub the garlic clove on the toasted bread slices.
- Spread the mixture on the bread and serve.

7.21 Spicy Nacho Chips

Preparation time: 15 mins

Servings: 24

Ingredients

- 12 cups unsalted nacho chips

- 6 tbsps. margarine
- 2 tbsps. low-sodium soy sauce
- 1tsp. powdered garlic
- 1 tsp. dried oregano
- 1/2 tsp. powder onion
- 1 tsp. smoked paprika
- 1 pinch hot pepper

Nutritional facts per serving

- Calories: 91cal
- Fat: 4g
- Sodium: 191mg
- Protein: 2g
- Potassium: 45mg
- Phosphorus: 26mg
- Carbohydrates: 15g

Steps

- Heat the oven to 250 °F.
- In a skillet, melt the margarine. Add all the seasoning and mix well.
- In a big bowl, toss the nacho chips with the seasoned margarine. Mix well co coat all the chips in the seasoning.
- Distribute the chips on a wide baking tray and bake for about 15 minutes.

7.22 Bannock Bread

Preparation time: 50 mins

Servings: 24

Ingredients

- 3 tsps. baking soda

- 5 cups water
- 1 cup and 2 tbsps. unsalted margarine
- 4 tsps. cream of tartar
- 10 cups white flour

Nutritional facts per serving

- Calories: 270cal
- Fat: 10g
- Sodium: 85mg
- Protein: 6g
- Potassium: 141mg
- Phosphorus: 58mg
- Carbohydrates: 41g

Steps

- Preheat the oven to 350°F.
- Stir all the dry ingredients together and add the water and 1 cup of melted margarine, little by little, kneading until you get a ball of dough.
- Cover with cling film and let rest for 30 minutes.
- Knead for 10 more minutes and divide the dough in 2 parts.
- Shape the dough balls into flat breads and put them into 2 10" round baking tins.
- With a wet knife, score the breads to cut into wedges.
- Bake the breads for 50 minutes or until they turn golden brown.
- Take the breads out of the oven and brush a little melted margarine on top.
- Let the breads cool and serve.

7.23 Homemade Pickles

Preparation time: 20 mins

Servings: 30

Ingredients

- 2 cups dill, chopped
- 1 tsp. black pepper
- 1 tsp. turmeric
- 2 cups white sugar
- 2 1/2cups rice vinegar
- 2 tsps. nigella seeds
- 5 big cucumbers
- 2 1/2 cups apple cider vinegar

- 1/2 tsp. dry mustard

Nutritional facts per serving

- Calories: 30cal
- Fat: 0g
- Sodium: 1mg
- Protein: 0g
- Potassium: 16mg
- Phosphorus: 2mg
- Carbohydrates: 9g

Steps

- Slice and divide the cucumbers into quart-sized jars, adding the nigella seeds and chopped dill between layers.
- Thoroughly whisk the sugar, turmeric, mustard, pepper and vinegars in a pitcher until the sugar is completely dissolved.
- Pour the mix in the jars, close and refrigerate for at least 1 month before serving.

7.24 Ginger Cranberry Cooler

Preparation time: 10 mins

Servings: 6

Ingredients

- 6 cups cranberry juice
- 6 tbsps. fresh ginger
- 1/2 cup fresh lime juice
- 1/2 cup granulated sugar

Nutritional facts per serving

- Calories: 125cal
- Fat: 0g
- Sodium: 1mg
- Protein: 1g
- Potassium: 51mg
- Phosphorus: 1mg
- Carbohydrates: 32g

Steps

- Thinly slice the fresh ginger.
- Bring to a simmer the cranberry juice and ginger in a pot, for about 20 minutes.
- Let cool, then add the lime juice and sugar, and whisk until the sugar dissolve
- Strain the drink and serve over ice in tall glasses.

CONCLUSION

Kidneys help you control the level of nutrients and minerals circulating in your body. When you experience kidney failure, your organs become unable to continue to perform this function well. As such, any doctor or dietician would definitely advise you to be careful in preparing your diet and ensuring that you are consuming enough (and not too much) protein, vitamins, and minerals. In this way, your kidneys will not struggle as much when filtering and removing waste from your blood. These recipes are great for anyone who is struggling with improving the health of his or her kidneys or managing a chronic kidney condition. Feel free to try out the ones that you find most appealing and embark on your journey to protecting your kidneys while improving your lifestyle.

Made in the USA
Middletown, DE
01 July 2021